The Complete Idiot's Reference Card

Recipes at a Glance

THE COMPLETE IDIOT'S GUIDE® TO

Cooking Soups

by Jenna Holst

alpha books

An Imprint of Macmillan General Reference
A Pearson Education Macmillan Company
1633 Broadway, New York, NY 10019-6785

Macmillan Publishing books may be purchased for business or sales promotional use. For information please write: Special Markets Department, Macmillan Publishing USA, 1633 Broadway, New York, NY 10019.

International Standard Book Number: 0-02-862861-6
Library of Congress Catalog Card Number: 9842080

01 00 99   8 7 6 5 4 3 2 1

Interpretation of the printing code: the rightmost number of the first series of numbers is the year of the book's printing; the rightmost number of the second series of numbers is the number of the book's printing. For example, a printing code of 99-1 shows that the first printing occurred in 1999.

Printed in the United States of America

Note: This publication contains the opinions and ideas of its author. It is intended to provide helpful and informative material on the subject matter covered. It is sold with the understanding that the author and publisher are not engaged in rendering professional services in the book. If the reader requires personal assistance or advice, a competent professional should be consulted.

The author and publisher specifically disclaim any responsibility for any liability, loss or risk, personal or otherwise, which is incurred as a consequence, directly or indirectly, of the use and application of any of the contents of this book.

Alpha Development Team

Publisher
Susan Clarey

Editorial Director
Anne Ficklen

Managing Editor
Bob Shuman

Marketing Brand Manager
Felice Primeau

Editor
Jim Willhite

Production Team

Production Editor
Suzanne Snyder

Copy Editor
Gail Burlakoff

Cover Designer
Mike Freeland

Photo Editor
Richard H. Fox

Illustrator
Kevin Spear
Eve Vaterlaus

Designer
Michele Laseau

Indexer
Johnna VanHoose

Layout/Proofreading
Ellen Considine
Pete Lippincott

Contents at a Glance

Contents

4 From the Garden 27

19 Cream Soups and Bisques 185

20 Chill Out 203

21 Fast Finishes 215

Appendix

Foreword

What turned me into a soup expert? My tireless passion for the stuff, any time, any day. My husband says my autobiography should be called *A Hundred Years of Soup*.

After creating hundreds of soup recipes for books, magazines and cooking classes over the last few years, I should feel burned out. Instead, leafing through the recipes in this book, I'm tempted by the Wild Rice and Mushroom Soup. I know it's good, so I'm hungry all over again for soup. I start to anticipate the precise moment, spoon in hand, when I take the plunge into that steaming bowl of soul-satisfying soup. But then, like a fleeting romance, it's all over when I turn the page and fall in love again, this time with Spiced Butternut Apple Soup.

If you have a passion for soup too, *The Complete Idiot's Guide to Soup* will ready you to embark on a love affair. This book literally holds your hand in the kitchen. Of course, coming from a long line of soup lovers, as I do, helps. My father always said, "I never met a bowl of soup I didn't like." And my great-grandmother, a Polish Jew, fed her large hungry family soup with every meal. One of her daughters, my Great Aunt Ida, now in her nineties, still gets misty-eyed every time she mentions her mother's hearty soups, like Beef-Barley, Hearty Pea, or Russian Sorrel Soup. But after you try a few of the comforting soups from from this book, you too will get misty-eyed when you remember them!

Don't cook much? Even if you have little time or ability for kitchen work you've bought the right book. Because, if there is just one dish you want to learn about, it has to be soup, because soup *IS* for idiots.

Soup is the most forgiving dish on the planet—just liquid and food in a happy marriage. Too thick? Add more liquid. Too thin? Boil it to evaporate the liquid. What you see is what you get and what you get is comfort, pleasure and flavors that get better over time.

Soup's versatile, durable nature counts for a lot in my life, as it will in yours. It reheats well, freezes and practically withstands the atom bomb—because, let's face it, even though I'm a professional, I'm fried at the end of the day too. And there's a hungry kid (and husband) who want dinner ten minutes ago. I do too. But my savior—soup—comes to the rescue. I yank it out of the freezer, fridge, or throw it together from almost no ingredients in just a few minutes. Ahhhhh, soup wins the weekday idiots' contest again and again.

Little equipment is required to make soup—a knife, a large pot and a ladle are a good start. If you like, stop there. But later on, when you get hooked on soup-making, you may want to purchase my favorite items: an inexpensive immersion blender to make your soup smooth right in the pot, and a degreasing pitcher to get rid of extra fat. All in all, I agree with Jenna that it is pointless to buy what you won't really use. Luckily, soup-making is a minimalist's dream.

Nothing in the house? This book will show you how to easily stock your pantry (even if is it the size of a postage stamp) with a few things that can be easily turned into soup. I like to keep potatoes and leeks on hand. In ten minutes they can be sliced, boiled in water (or stock), seasoned with salt and freshly ground pepper then finished off with a pat of butter. Another favorite of mine is beans, both canned or dried, because it takes so little effort to make a superb soup with them. Make sure to stock fresh garlic, some oils and vinegars and few dried herbs and spices too. (A good curry powder, rosemary, and cumin are some of my favorites.) Soon, accompanied with some crusty bread, pantry items turn themselves into dinner.

Once you're comfortable making soup, check out Jenna's inspired chapter on improvising you own. Because some of the most satisfying soups start with a few fresh, seasonal items that catch your eye—asparagus in the spring, root vegetables in the winter, corn and tomatoes in the summer. After a short simmering, their aromas will lure you to the table to devour a bowl of your own homemade soup.
—Amy Cotler

Amy Cotler is a cookbook author and cooking teacher who developed soups and stocks for *The Joy of Cooking*. She hosts a cooking forum for "The *New York Times* on The Web," and Peter Kump's School of Culinary Arts.

Introduction

Soup has long been recognized as a nutritious food that comforts and restores both body and soul. A pot of simmering soup on the stove typifies the warmth of home and hearth. It makes us feel good. Yet soup has not always been the symbol of home cooking. The first restaurants were located in Paris (but of course!) in the late 1700s and served only warming and hearty soups, which even then were believed to have restorative powers. The word restaurant itself is derived from the French word *restaurer*, meaning to restore and refresh.

Soups are often inexpensive and generally quite easy to prepare. Make a batch—and regenerate, renew, and restore yourself and your family and friends.

You'll discover that making soup is easy, rewarding, and fun, and you end up with a great meal! This book is divided into five parts that guide you through all the aspects of soup preparation. It's filled with down-to-earth advice and fascinating information as well as obvious and not-so-obvious cooking tips. The book travels full circle, beginning in your kitchen, then heading out to the market, and finally returning to your kitchen where you can cook and savor the delectable homemade soups of diverse cultures.

How to Use this Book

Part 1, The Soup Kitchen, provides practical suggestions on setting up your kitchen so you'll know which essential cooking tools and staple food items to keep on hand. You'll have what you need, but you won't waste space or money on things you don't need.

Part 2, Alphabet Soup: The Basic Ingredients, holds your formal introduction to the building blocks of soup: the ingredients—from veggies to dairy, meat, poultry, and seafood. Although you might be familiar with some, others might be new to you. You'll learn how to use them in soups, which can be different than using them in other dishes. There's also a chapter on seasonings—herbs and spices and the flavorings that make the recipes and your soup especially tasty.

Part 3, The Souper Chef, is the essence of soup cookery. You'll learn about *mise en place* (how to set up before starting cooking), cooking techniques, what broth to use, and why things are done a certain way, as well as food safety procedures. The final chapter, "Playing with Your Food," explains how to substitute ingredients and improvise so can you lend your individual touch to a recipe or make your own simple soup.

Part 4, From the Ladle to the Table, offers advice on how to serve soup, from menu hints, to what bowls to use, to garnishes. You'll be serving like a pro.

Part 5, The Recipes, is what you've been waiting for. In these eight chapters you'll find updated recipes for delicious classic, ethnic, and innovative soups. You're bound to find a few favorites among them. You'll also master the secrets of homemade broth.

Many of the recipes are very easy to make, although a few are more challenging. The level of ease or difficulty, ballpark preparation and cooking times, special equipment needs (such as a food processor or blender), and whether a certain soup is freezer-worthy are indicated also.

Extras

In addition to instructions, explanations, and recipes, each chapter of the book features several sidebars that offer fun facts as well as practical advice. You'll come to recognize each by its unique icon.

Souper Bowl Fact

These sidebars contain interesting tidbits, lore, and information about a particular soup, ingredient, or equipment.

Souper Saver

These sidebars are cautions. They'll help you prevent mistakes or warn you against doing things that might cause a problem.

Souper Clue

These sidebars are culinary tips and commonsense hints to make your cooking easier, more productive, and enjoyable.

Souper Idea

These sidebars are suggestions. They present minor adjustments to alter a recipe, such as changing the flavor or texture, and offer ingredient substitutions. You end up with more than one way to make a particular soup.

Acknowledgments

Many thanks to Pieto, Ansa, Jim Willhite, and Jane Dystel.

Part 1
The Soup Kitchen

Your kitchen is your culinary laboratory and, like any work space, it needs to be set up properly. In this section, you'll discover how to outfit your kitchen with equipment that's not only great for making soup, but that also can do double duty and be used to prepare many other meals. Kitchenware is an investment. You don't need lots of specialized tools, but a few quality items that will see you through. You'll also find out what food to keep in stock—on your shelves as well as in your fridge and freezer. Having a well-equipped kitchen will make a tremendous difference in the way you cook and perhaps even in how often you cook.

Chapter 1

Tooling Up

In This Chapter

➤ What to look for when you buy pots

➤ Which kitchen knives, gadgets, and utensils are really necessary

➤ A quick look at appliances and how they perform

Having the right tools makes the time you spend in the kitchen more effective and efficient, but with the abundance of kitchen products on the market what exactly do you need? Before buying anything, ask yourself a few questions: Do I really need this? Will I use it? Is it well made? Will it last?

Soup doesn't require too much equipment—on the most basic level a knife, a cutting board, a large pot with a lid, a wooden spoon and a ladle, and maybe an old-fashioned food-mill for purees. Those are the tools our grandmothers used, and they work well. Modern cooks have more choices, and there are several items that make cooking easier and more enjoyable.

Pots and Pans

Pots and pans don't need to be expensive, but they should be well made. Select those with tight-fitting lids and ovenproof handles that are securely attached with rivets, screws, or sturdy welding. Soup pots should be a medium- to heavy-gauge metal with a thick bottom, so that the heat stays evenly distributed and food doesn't scorch. Thin-bottomed pots warp more easily and get hot spots where food invariably burns, no matter how low the heat source. Make sure that you'll be able to comfortably lift the pot even when it's filled with soup. Pots can last a lifetime, so consider your options and buy the best quality within your budget.

What You Need

➤ 4$^1/_2$- to 6-quart heavy Dutch oven with lid

➤ 1$^1/_2$-quart saucepan with lid

➤ 2$^1/_2$- to 3-quart saucepan with lid

➤ 10-inch skillet (the Dutch oven's lid may fit)

➤ 8- to 10-quart stock pot with lid (optional)

Souper Saver

Nonstick surfaces help you reduce the amount of fat you use and can be ideal for some people. However, if the coating is cracked, flaking, or peeling, don't use the pot—replace it.

The best choices are enameled cast iron, stainless steel with an aluminum core or thick aluminum bottom, and medium- to heavy-weight enameled pots, because they retain heat well. Aluminum, although an excellent heat conductor, reacts with food, particularly acidic foods such as tomatoes, and can impart a metallic taste if food is left in the pot too long after cooking. Anodized aluminum pots are a medium gray color and have been treated so there is less reaction with food. Plain cast iron needs to be well seasoned to prevent rusting. It, too, can react slightly with acidic foods.

stock pot

dutch oven

Souper Bowl Fact

Stock pots are tall and narrow, with straight sides, and are used for making stock or broth. Dutch ovens are shorter and wider, sometimes with slightly curved sides, and are perfect for making soups and stews. You can also use them to make smaller batches of broth.

Knives

A sharp knife is a cook's best friend. You'll need only three to four knives, and if you buy good quality, knives, like other kitchen tools, should last for years. Ideally the blade should be high-carbon stainless steel, which keeps a sharp edge longer than ordinary stainless steel. Knives should feel good in your hand and not be too big or unwieldy for you to work with. Follow your gut instinct on this one, not friends' or salespeople's recommendations. Knives should be well-balanced and have handles that are securely riveted or attached. Store them in a knife block or on a knife rack so they'll stay sharp. If you toss them in a drawer, they'll become dull more quickly.

What You Need

> ➤ 3- to 4-inch paring knife
> ➤ 6- to 8-inch chef's knife for chopping
> ➤ Serrated knife for slicing bread and tomatoes
> ➤ 8- to 10-inch slicing knife, optional
> ➤ Sharpening steel
> ➤ Sharpening stone or knife sharpener
> ➤ Carving or large kitchen fork

paring knife

chef's knife

You must care for your knives. To do this effectively, you'll need both a sharpening stone (or an electric or nonelectric sharpening machine) as well as a steel. A steel straightens the edge of the knife but doesn't actually sharpen it. Try to use the steel at least once or twice a week. If your knife is only a bit dull, the edge probably isn't straight. Often a few strokes on a steel can restore it. Once a month you should sharpen your knives, then pass them on the steel. Serrated knives don't need to be maintained this way. If a serrated blade doesn't cut well anymore, it should be replaced.

If you're unsure how to use any of the cutlery or sharpening equipment, ask the salesperson at a cookware shop or a knowledgeable friend to demonstrate the proper technique. Have them watch you do it so they can guide you. It's important that you learn to use these instruments correctly and safely. I know this sounds like monkey see, monkey do—it is. How-to drawings in books or magazines can give you the proper idea, but there's nothing better than actually watching someone with skill and then repeating their action.

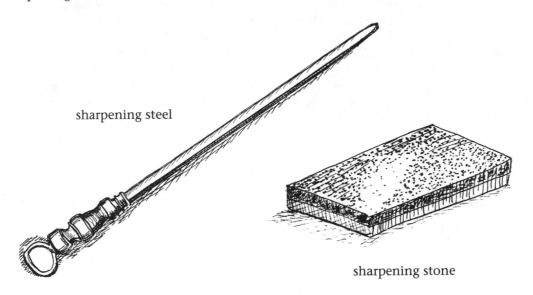

sharpening steel

sharpening stone

Essential Utensils

There are zillions of gadgets and utensils on the market. Some are excellent, time-cutting tools, but many of them are expensive fads, things you'll use a few times and then never use again.

What You Need: Basic Equipment

➤ Baking sheet

➤ Can and bottle opener

➤ Colander

- ➤ Cooling rack
- ➤ Cutting boards
- ➤ Grater, preferably four-sided
- ➤ Measuring-cup set, for both dry and liquid ingredients
- ➤ Measuring spoons
- ➤ Mixing bowls
- ➤ Sieves, medium diameter, 1 fine mesh and 1 medium mesh
- ➤ Storage containers with covers for freezer and refrigerator, and/or self-sealing plastic bags for storage

Souper Saver

Cuts happen more often with dull knives than with sharp ones because you have to work harder and exert more pressure on the blade to slice or chop properly. A sharp knife requires less effort on your part. Let a sharp blade do more of the work for you.

Utensils

- ➤ Ladle
- ➤ Skimmer
- ➤ Spoons, wooden, slotted, and solid
- ➤ Tongs
- ➤ Vegetable peeler
- ➤ Wine opener

In addition to these items you'll need a supply of aluminum foil, freezer paper, paper towels, plastic wrap, and self-sealing plastic bags.

Hand and Electric Appliances

You don't need many, but your soup kitchen will be complete if you own one or two of these handy tools. Buy what you'll use on a fairly regular basis or what you honestly think you can't do without.

Hand Blender

This is a wonderful appliance. It's convenient, portable, and very easy to use. Plug it in, immerse the blade end in the food you want to puree, and switch on the power. Move the blender around the pot until the desired texture is achieved. It can create a chunky or fairly fine texture. Sometimes a few chunks of food escape the blades. You might want to feel for them by slowly stirring the soup with a wooden spoon, and then using the hand blender again in that area. Vegetables must be very soft for this product to perform at its best. Clean-up is a breeze—wash only the blade end in soapy water, and rinse.

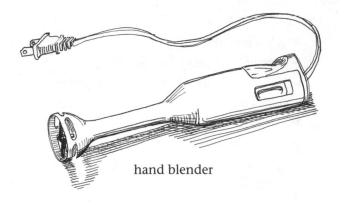

hand blender

Food Processor

The modern kitchen's workhorse, a food processor can be used for everything from making pastry to shredding cabbage. Fitted with the steel blade, it is good for pureeing thick soups as well as for chopping onions. The texture it produces is not as smooth as what you'll get with a blender or hand blender. To compensate, you might want to strain the solid ingredients and puree them in batches with a little of the broth, then combine them afterward. The end result definitely will have a finer texture.

Blender

This all-around tool has been on the market for years. It is fine for fairly thin pureed soups such as carrot or tomato, but it doesn't work as well for thicker purees such as beans or lentils. If you use a blender, always puree in batches, filling the container only one-third full. Start the blender at a low speed and then, while it's running, adjust it to a higher level. If it's too full, the soup will leak out, and if it's hot, you can get burned.

Food Mill

Grandma's forerunner to the food processor, this nonelectric tool often has interchangeable discs that can be used for shredding as well as pureeing to various textures, depending on which blade you use. To use it for purees for soups, the vegetables must be very soft. Food mills puree and strain simultaneously, taking out skins and undercooked vegetables as well as seeds, which makes it a good choice for tomato and berry purees.

food mill

Spice Mill

Hand spice mills look like large pepper mills, with a crankshaft and opening on top for loading the whole spices and a container below to catch the ground spices. They're easy to use and can be found in good cookware shops. If you prefer to use an electric spice mill, choose a small, inexpensive coffee grinder that you earmark for spices only. Partially fill the container with spices, turn on the power, and in a matter of seconds they'll be freshly ground.

The Least You Need to Know

➤ A good pot has a thick base and conducts heat evenly.

➤ Keep knives sharp! A dull knife is more dangerous because it requires more force.

➤ When pureeing, don't overfill the blender or food processor bowl. Instead, puree in batches.

Stocking Up

Having a variety of ingredients in-house makes shopping and cooking easier. It also gives you greater flexibility and can spark your culinary imagination. Sometimes you'll already have everything you need in stock so you won't have to dash out and shop, but can start cooking right away.

Supply your kitchen with foods you like and use often, of course, but add a few exotic spices, condiments, or ethnic ingredients. You don't need to keep more than one or two of each item on your shelves unless you cook with it regularly, such as canned tomatoes or broth. It's helpful to keep a grocery list handy in your kitchen so you can mark down whether you need to replace any staples you've used.

In Your Kitchen Cabinets

Years ago, items with a long shelf life were stored in a separate pantry that was located off the kitchen. Few of us have pantries anymore. Instead, we keep these items in our kitchen cupboards.

What You Need

- ➤ Apple juice
- ➤ Barley, pearled
- ➤ Beans, an assortment of dried and canned
- ➤ Broth, low-sodium chicken and beef
- ➤ Clams, canned
- ➤ Clam juice
- ➤ Crackers
- ➤ Flour, all-purpose
- ➤ Lentils, brown
- ➤ Mussels, canned or bottled
- ➤ Olive oil
- ➤ Pasta, an assortment of shapes
- ➤ Peanut butter, natural style
- ➤ Rice, white, basmati, brown, and wild
- ➤ Salmon, canned
- ➤ Salad dressing
- ➤ Sugar, white and brown
- ➤ Tomatoes, assorted canned varieties: whole plum, chopped, pureed
- ➤ Tomato paste, preferably small cans or in a resealable tube
- ➤ Vegetable oil, such as peanut, safflower, or corn

In A Cool, Dry Place

Most of these staples you'll use almost every day, but a few might be reserved for special recipes. Except for dried mushrooms, which I keep in a self-sealing plastic bag, I like to keep these items in a fairly dark spot where there is some air circulation around them so they don't spoil or grow sprouts. They can be stored in a basket, cabinet, or drawer.

What You Need

- ➤ Garlic
- ➤ Mushrooms, dried (such as shiitake or porcini)
- ➤ Onions
- ➤ Potatoes

➤ Sweet Potatoes

➤ Winter squash, such as butternut or acorn

In Your Fridge

You won't need every one of these items, but here's a list of what's helpful to have at your fingertips. Whatever I don't use too often—such as half-and-half, cream, butter-milk, or highly perishable items—I buy when it's called for in a recipe. The same goes for most fragile, fresh produce such as mushrooms, lettuce, green beans, spinach, and the like. Although parsley and lemons don't last long, they're so versatile and used so often for both flavoring and garnishing in everything from soups to salads to entrees that it's advisable to have them on hand.

What You Need: Dairy

➤ Butter or margarine

➤ Eggs

➤ Milk or low-fat milk

➤ Sour cream or nonfat sour cream

➤ Yogurt, preferably low-fat

What You Need: Produce

➤ Apples

➤ Carrots

➤ Celery

➤ Bell peppers

➤ Ginger, fresh, 2- to 3-inch piece

➤ Lemons

➤ Oranges

➤ Parsley

➤ Scallions

In Your Freezer

If you have a small freezer, only keep on hand what you think you'll use in a month or so. If you have a large freezer compartment or a separate appliance, keep a good supply of ingredients at your disposal.

What You Need

➤ Beef bottom round or chuck, cubed

➤ Bread or rolls

➤ Broccoli or cauliflower florets

➤ Corn kernels

➤ Chicken parts or boneless chicken pieces

➤ Green beans

➤ Lima beans

➤ Oxtail

➤ Peas

➤ Shrimp

➤ Spinach, chopped or whole

Souper Clue

You can freeze butter or margarine for several months. Wrap it well in plastic wrap or put it in a self-sealing bag so that it doesn't develop freezer burn and taste slightly off.

Seasoning

It's commonplace for cooks to use an array of seasonings from around the world. Your cabinet will reflect the diversity of your personal culinary taste. Don't rush out and fill the spice rack. Buy what you use frequently. Otherwise, buy seasonings as you need them for a specific recipe. Here's a list of the flavorful ingredients used in the soup recipes.

What You MAY Need: Spices

➤ Allspice (whole berries and ground)

➤ Caraway seeds

➤ Cardamom (whole and ground)

➤ Cayenne or ground red chili pepper

➤ Cloves (whole and ground)

➤ Chili powder

➤ Crushed red chili flakes

➤ Cinnamon (sticks and ground)

➤ Coriander (ground or whole)

➤ Cumin (ground)

➤ Curry powder, preferably Madras style

➤ Mustard, dried English style

➤ Nutmeg, preferably whole so it can be freshly grated on the small side of a grater; otherwise, ground

➤ Paprika and Hungarian sweet paprika

➤ Black peppercorns (to be freshly ground)

➤ White pepper, ground (or white peppercorns if you have a mill specifically for white pepper)

➤ Turmeric

What You MAY Need: Herbs

➤ Basil

➤ Bay leaf

➤ Chives

➤ Cilantro (use only fresh)

➤ Dill, preferably fresh

➤ Mint, preferably fresh

➤ Oregano

➤ Parsley, preferably flat-leaf (use only fresh)

➤ Rosemary

➤ Thyme leaves

Souper Saver

Seal spices, herbs, or condiments after opening to keep them fresh. Check condiment labels to see whether they need to be refrigerated after opening.

What You MAY Need: Significant Others

➤ Dijon mustard

➤ Chinese sesame oil

➤ Chinese chili oil

➤ Salt, kosher, fine-grained, or sea salt

➤ Sherry

➤ Soy sauce

➤ Tabasco or other liquid hot red pepper sauce

➤ Thai fish sauce

➤ Vermouth, dry white

➤ Wine vinegar, rice wine, and white wine

➤ Worcestershire sauce

The Least You Need to Know

➤ Stock your kitchen cabinets with items that you use often.

➤ Keep potatoes, onions, garlic, and other semiperishables in a cool, dry place.

➤ Check your fridge and freezer before shopping—you might already have everything you need.

Part 2
Alphabet Soup:
The Basic Ingredients

Do you know what to look for in a tomato? One that has smooth skin and firm flesh? How about in a chicken? And what's the best way to keep herbs fresh? If you want to make good soup, you've got to get on more than speaking terms with things you formerly passed by or took for granted—you need know them in depth. The chapters in this section will give you intimate knowledge of ordinary and exotic food from the garden to the spice shelf and everything in between.

Chapter 3

Off the Shelf

In This Chapter

➤ The low-down on beans

➤ Learning about rice

➤ What pasta is best in soup

➤ Olive and other oils

All the ingredients highlighted in this chapter have a long shelf life, which means you can buy them in bulk and not worry about them going bad quickly. Most should be kept in a sealed container in a cool, dry place such as a kitchen cupboard or cabinet.

Canned goods, such as tomatoes, fish, and broth, are the most commonly stored items. All cans should be undented because dents sometimes conceal small holes, invisible to the eye, through which airborne bacteria can enter and cause the food inside to spoil. Sometimes labels have use-by dates, so check for them.

There's an abundance of other shelf-stable items that aren't processed or canned that are perfect for soup. These include dried food such as pastas, rice, and legumes, as well as vegetable oils.

Legumes: Beans, Lentils, and Split Peas

Always marvelous in soup, inexpensive, and nutritious, legumes can be purchased in one- or two-pound bags at the supermarket, or loose in many health food or ethnic grocery stores. If you buy them in bags, store them that way, but if you buy in bulk, keep them in sealed glass or plastic containers. Either way, they will last in your cabinet for a year or more. The varieties of beans are numerous, but here's a compendium of those that are called for in the recipes.

Black Beans

Widely used in Latin American, Mexican, and Caribbean cuisine, black beans are kidney shaped and actually have a white flesh. Their rich and earthy taste can stand up to hot chilies, spices, and garlic.

Chickpeas

Also known as garbanzo beans, these round, irregularly shaped beans have a mild, nutty flavor. They are used in soups, salads, and stews of Mediterranean countries such as Spain, Italy, Morocco, and the Middle East as well as in recipes from Latin America and India.

Pinto Beans

These kidney-shaped beans are beige or pink and dotted with dark brown flecks. They are used in southwestern, Tex-Mex, and Mexican foods.

Red Kidney Beans, Small Red Beans, and Pink Beans

These meaty beans can be used interchangeably and may be substituted when pinto beans are called for. Although not traditional, they can replace white beans in minestrone.

White Beans

There are many kinds of white beans, all having a mild flavor and somewhat creamy texture. Use Great Northern, Navy, or white kidney (also called by their Italian name, cannellini) beans interchangeably.

Brown Lentils

These are the common lentils sold everywhere and are suitable for the soup recipes. The smaller French green lentils and red lentils are not a substitute.

Split Peas

Green peas have an intense pea taste but their yellow cousins are somewhat milder. Both are most often found split, although you can find them whole in some markets.

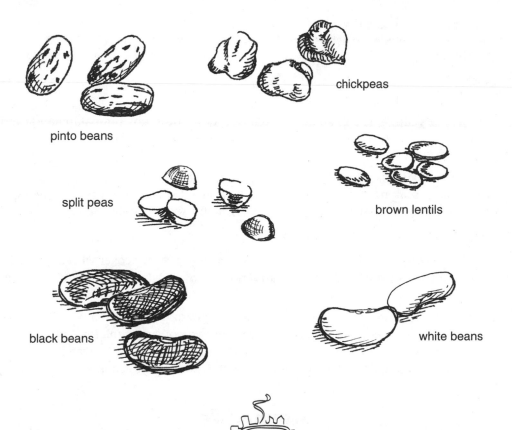

pinto beans

chickpeas

split peas

brown lentils

black beans

white beans

Souper Bowl Fact

Here are some legume equivalents:

➤ 1 pound dried beans = 2 to $2^1/_2$ cups uncooked, and becomes $6^1/_2$ to $7^1/_2$ cups when cooked.

➤ 1 pound dried lentils or split peas = $2^1/_2$ cups uncooked, and becomes 7 to $7^1/_2$ cups when cooked.

➤ One 15- to 16-ounce can, rinsed and drained = $1^1/_2$ to $1^3/_4$ cups cooked beans.

➤ One 20-ounce can, rinsed and drained = 2 cups.

Sorting Beans

Pebbles are often hidden amongst the beans. To prevent a cracked tooth, you must sort through them.

Put the beans in a colander and rinse under cold running water. Pick through to remove any pebbles or debris as well as any discolored and shriveled beans.

Presoaking

To soak or not to soak, that is the question. No matter what the color—red, green, brown, or yellow—lentils and dried split peas don't need any presoaking and can be used after they have been washed and picked over. Whole dried peas do benefit from soaking, however.

I nearly always soak dried beans. Although some respected, modern chefs don't see the advantage, soaking does remove a percentage, albeit small, of the gas-producing sugars that can cause digestive problems and bloating for some people.

There are two methods of soaking:

➤ **Overnight Method:** Put the beans in a large pot and cover with approximately 3 inches of water above the beans and soak overnight. Drain and cover again with fresh water to cook.

➤ **Quick Method:** Put the beans in a large pot and cover them with 2 to 3 inches of water. Over high heat, bring the water to a boil and cook for 2 minutes. Remove the pot from the heat and let the beans stand in the water for 1 hour before using. Drain and cover again with fresh water to cook.

Souper Saver

When cooking fresh legumes, adding salt or acidic foods such as tomatoes, vinegar, or wine can make them toughen and take much longer to cook. Add these ingredients to the pot after the beans are already tender. Simmer a while longer until their flavors are fully incorporated.

Canned Beans

Although their texture is somewhat softer than that of freshly cooked dried beans, they are time-saving, convenient, and will still make a good soup. Before using, put the canned beans in a sieve or colander and pour off any of the canning liquid. Rinse them well under cold, running water and drain.

Rice

Rice is one of the world's most popular dietary staples and is a welcome addition to soup. It too has a long shelf life when stored correctly. If you plan to use rice often you can keep it in its box; otherwise, once opened, transfer it to a container.

Rice is porous and absorbs other flavors that it comes in contact with. Make sure you don't store it near your spices or it may end up tasting like curry powder or cinnamon. But this trait has its benefits too, and can transform ordinary rice into a luxury item. Flavor your rice by storing it with a dried wild mushroom (or two) such as a morel or porcini or, if you're extravagant, a truffle—ooh la la. This is particularly good for Arborio rice that's used for risotto. Note that the truffle or mushroom can still be utilized in another dish. Store flavored rice in a sealed glass or plastic container and label it.

There are several types of rice suitable for soup, and here's a handy guide.

White Rice

White rice is polished, which means the germ and bran have been removed. There are basically two types of white rice: long-grain, whose grains remain separate after cooking, and short-grain, whose grains stick together after cooking. Use all-purpose, long-grain white rice for most soups where white rice is specified. For a nuttier taste, try basmati or Texmati. Jasmine, the sweet-tasting Thai rice, and Arborio, the popular short-grain white rice used in risotto, are not appropriate for the soup recipes. White rice takes between 15 and 20 minutes to cook.

Souper Clue

The Raw and the Cooked: Although this might seem obvious, I've been asked this question several times. When uncooked or raw rice is called for, the recipe will simply call for X amount of "rice," but when cooked rice is required, it will specify X amount of "cooked rice."

Brown Rice

This is unmilled or unpolished rice and is slightly more nutritious than white rice because the germ and bran are intact. It has a richer taste and firmer texture and takes about 45 to 55 minutes to cook. Quick brown rice, which takes about 15 to 20 minutes to cook, is also available in many markets, and this type can be substituted for white rice in soup because their cooking times are similar. In recipes where cooked rice is called for you may substitute cooked brown rice.

Wild Rice

Not really rice, but the seed of a wild marsh grass, wild rice is often combined with white or brown rice. It has a unique, nutty taste that is wonderful with mushrooms. The cooking time is between 50 to 60 minutes. Do not substitute wild rice for other rice in soup.

Barley

Cultivated and eaten since the Stone Age, this delicious and filling grain is rich in both protein and B vitamins. Although not specifically a rice, barley fulfills a similar function in soup. Pearled or pearl barley is the type most readily available. Although its bran has been removed for easier and shorter cooking, it still has good nutritional value. Stored in an airtight container, pearled barley should last for 9 to 12 months and sometimes longer.

Pasta

In soup, you'll probably use dried pastas or noodles instead of freshly made. Stored in a cool, dry place, dried pasta will keep almost indefinitely. Noodles or pasta rarely need to be prepared separately, but are added directly to the soup and cooked. Small shapes or miniature pasta, as opposed to long noodles, are most often called for in soup. Use small shells, small elbow macaroni, *ditalini* (small tubes), thin egg noodles, wide egg noodles, or *tortellini* as required.

Naturally, there's an exception to this rule—Asian noodle soups require long, ramen-style noodles. If the noodles are too long for you to eat comfortably, you can break them before cooking. Other Asian noodles sometimes used in soup are rice noodles or rice sticks. These have a short cooking time, and you must adjust the timing in recipes accordingly if you substitute these noodles in any of the Asian soup recipes in this book. Mung bean noodles, also called bean threads, must be soaked in a bowl of hot water for about 20 minutes and drained. They then can be added directly to fully cooked soup right before serving.

Olive and Other Vegetable Oils

Olive oil is considered one of the most healthful of all oils. A staple of Mediterranean cuisine, it is a must for any kitchen. Wonderful in cooking and in dressings, its color can range from deep green to pale gold. The less refined the oil, such as the extra virgin olive oil yielded by the first pressing, then the stronger the flavor and the higher the cost. There are many grades of olive oil on the market and you need to be aware of what you're buying and how it's best used. The most expensive, most flavorful extra virgin olive oils are best used as a flavoring and not as a cooking oil. Sometimes another vegetable oil is a better choice. Peanut and olive oil have a high burn point, which means either is good for sautéing. Other frequently used oils include corn, safflower, and canola. Store them in a cool cupboard.

Olive oil is a monounsaturated fat, believed to help reduce the LDL or bad cholesterol levels in your blood. Canola is the next highest oil in terms of mono-unsaturated fats, and peanut oil is about half mono-unsaturated. Polyunsaturated fats include corn, soy, safflower, and sesame oils. Although healthier than hydrogenated fats, such as margarine, or saturated fats, such as butter, they possess no cholesterol-lowering properties.

Souper Clue

If you live where it's very hot and humid, you might want to keep cooking oils in the refrigerator in summer. They can go off and taste rancid. Always store oils that you don't often use, especially strong-flavored oils such as Chinese toasted sesame oil, in the fridge.

Here's a breakdown of commonly used oils:

➤ **Extra virgin olive oil** comes from the first pressing and tends to have a strong, fruity aroma and taste. It should be reserved for salad dressings, pesto, and as a condiment for drizzling on fish, pasta, vegetables, and chicken.

➤ **Virgin olive oil** comes from the second pressing and has a milder, yet rich, full-bodied taste. It is perfect for sautéing most items.

➤ **Pure olive oil** is more refined, and although it's not as flavorful, it can still be used for sautéing.

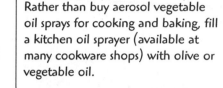

Souper Clue

Rather than buy aerosol vegetable oil sprays for cooking and baking, fill a kitchen oil sprayer (available at many cookware shops) with olive or vegetable oil.

➤ **Extra-light olive oil** is heavily processed and extremely mild and pale. Don't be fooled—it doesn't have less calories than other oils, just less taste. Use another, cheaper vegetable oil instead.

➤ **Vegetable oils** such as *canola, safflower, corn,* and *peanut* range in color from yellow to gold and are flavorless. They are excellent all-purpose oils for general cooking and are less expensive than olive oil. They can be used interchangeably, although it's worth noting that canola oil has the highest level of monounsaturated fat.

The Least You Need to Know

➤ Wash and pick over all legumes before using.

➤ Properly stored, legumes, rice, and dried pasta will last almost indefinitely. Keep these ingredients in a cool, dry place, preferably in a sealed glass or plastic container.

➤ Cook with virgin olive oil for full-bodied flavor; otherwise, use flavorless canola, peanut, safflower, or corn oils.

Chapter 4

From the Garden

> ## In This Chapter
>
> ➤ Discover the abundant produce in the marketplace.
>
> ➤ Learn which varieties are best in soups.
>
> ➤ Find out how to prep produce for cooking and storage.

Produce is the essence of many fine soups, generating either a pleasingly straight-forward taste or layers of subtly complex flavor. High-quality vegetables and fruit are fundamental to any good cooking. Although most items are available year-round in supermarkets and specialty stores, items that are out of season can be of lesser caliber and more costly. Locally grown items are seasonal, and seasonal produce is what nearly always tastes best.

Price is a good indicator of what's in season. Tomatoes, for example, are more expensive in winter than in summer. Canned tomatoes or frozen veggies can be preferable when fresh isn't appealing or is beyond your budget. Farmers' markets and roadside stalls are marvelous places to shop for the freshest homegrown produce.

Seasonal Produce Summary

This convenient reference will let you know when it is prime time for a particular item, even those that are on the shelves throughout the year:

> ➤ **Spring and Summer:** Asparagus, Bell Peppers, Berries, Corn, Cucumbers, Eggplant, Garden Peas, New Potatoes, String and Wax Beans, Sugar Snap Peas, Snow Peas, Spinach, Tomatoes, and Zucchini

➤ **Winter:** Acorn Squash, Butternut Squash, Apples, Beets, Broccoli, Cabbage, Carrots, Cauliflower, Leeks, Onions, Parsnips, Pears, Potatoes, Pumpkin, Rutabaga, Sweet Potatoes, and Turnips

➤ **Year-round:** Bell Peppers, Carrots, Celery, Cantaloupe, Lettuce, Mushrooms, Onions, Potatoes, Radishes, Scallions, Spinach, Sweet Potatoes

No matter when or where you buy them, it's important to select fresh, unblemished items with smooth, uncracked skin. When you're making soup, however, if some of your leftover veggies have a few dark patches or softer spots, you can cut them out. Of course if the vegetables are rotten, moldy, smell strongly, or taste off, don't even think of using them—throw them out.

Souper Saver

Too much moisture causes decay, so don't wash produce before storing it in the refrigerator. Pat it dry if it's been misted in the store.

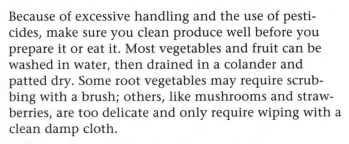

Souper Clue

Grown in sandy soil, asparagus requires thorough washing. Soak it in a sink filled with cold water. Let it stand for several minutes, so the dirt loosens and sinks. Repeat the process until you're satisfied that it's clean.

Because of excessive handling and the use of pesticides, make sure you clean produce well before you prepare it or eat it. Most vegetables and fruit can be washed in water, then drained in a colander and patted dry. Some root vegetables may require scrubbing with a brush; others, like mushrooms and strawberries, are too delicate and only require wiping with a clean damp cloth.

There's a whole world of vegetables and fruit to explore. Here are some that make great soup.

Apples and Pears

These two fruits are delectable additions to many soups, both sweet and savory. There are numerous apple and pear varieties. Select fruit that is firm and unblemished. For apples, I prefer to cook with Cortland, Granny Smith, Delicious, MacIntosh, and Rome; for pears, I prefer Bosc, Bartlett, or Anjou.

Both pears and apples should be peeled and cored before they're used in soup. Because the flesh turns brown, you might want to put the fruit in a bowl of acidulated water until you're ready to use it.

Asparagus

Choose firm spears that are uniform in size with tightly closed tips. Break off the bottom of the stalk where it bends—you shouldn't cut it with a knife. If the stems are large, make sure you peel them to about $1/2$ inch from the tip. Thin stalks rarely need peeling. Refrigerated, asparagus will keep for 3 to 5 days.

Souper Bowl Fact

Acidulated water is water to which a small amount of lemon or lime juice has been added. Put cut fruit such as apples and pears or vegetables such as artichokes in a bowl of acidulated water to keep the flesh from discoloring.

Avocados

Native to tropical and subtropical climates, avocados were once called alligator pears. Haas, the one with the rough skin, has superior flavor, and I prefer it to its smooth-skinned counterpart, called Fuerte. A ripe avocado should give when you press on it, but not be squishy. Buy them as you need them and store them at room temperature—65 to 75 degrees. If you have several that have ripened simultaneously, you can refrigerate them for a couple of days to keep them from becoming too soft.

Beans

There are many kinds of beans, but in soups you will most often use ordinary string beans and lima beans. String beans should be bright green, firm, and snap when you break them. For a change you can substitute wax beans. Snap off the end of the bean where it was attached to the plant, not the tip. Beans can be sliced on an angle or in small pieces. Frozen string beans are just fine, but don't use canned, which lack texture and flavor.

Fresh lima beans are often hard to find, but if you are so fortunate, they should be medium size in the pod, and the pod should snap crisply when broken. Fortunately, frozen lima beans are plentiful and can be used successfully in any recipe. It's up to you whether you use regular or baby limas.

Souper Clue

To ripen hard avocados, put them in a sealed paper bag or wrap them in newspaper. In a day or two they should be ripe.

Beets

Beets are a sweet-tasting, ruby-colored root vegetable. If available, buy them with the leaves attached, but cut or twist off the tops before you store them in the refrigerator. (Save the tops to cook as greens.) They're also sold without tops and prepacked in bags. Fresh beets can last in your fridge for about 3 weeks. When beets are used in soup, they tend to dominate in flavor and turn any broth red, not to mention your hands.

➤ **Cooking time for beets:** 35 to 40 minutes for medium beets; 60 minutes or more for large beets.

➤ **To peel beets easily:** After cooking place them in a colander in the sink under cold running water or plunge them into a sink of cold water. Slice off the stem end of the beet. The skin should slip off easily if the beets are thoroughly cooked.

Souper Idea

Beet greens can be cooked like spinach and served as a delightful and nutritious side dish. Uncooked, they will last about 3 days in your fridge.

Bell Peppers

Look for peppers with smooth skin that are firm when pressed gently. Green, red, and yellow peppers are available year-round. Domestic bell peppers are generally less expensive than imported ones and are equally good. You can substitute red for yellow.

To prepare bell peppers, cut out the stem and remove the seeds. Slice the peppers in half lengthwise and trim off the inner membranes, then cut as directed.

Broccoli, Cabbage, and Cauliflower

All members of the cabbage family, these vegetables should be firm to the touch. Broccoli should have tight green florets and a rigid stem; cabbage should feel heavy for its size and have tight leaves; cauliflower should be off-white with little discoloration and have compact florets.

There are several types of cabbage: green, savoy, red, and Chinese or bok choy. Most of the soup recipes call for green or savoy. Some markets cut large cabbages into wedges. This is a good buy if you don't need a lot. Note, however, that cabbages can be kept in the refrigerator for 2 to 3 weeks.

Souper Clue

Separate broccoli and cauliflower into florets before washing.

When it comes to broccoli and cauliflower, try to purchase the whole piece of broccoli, with stems intact, or the entire head of cauliflower, instead of a few florets. The stems are quite flavorful and excellent for soup. Both can be stored in the refrigerator for about 5 days.

Cantaloupes

American cantaloupes are actually muskmelons. They are low in calories, high in fiber, and an excellent source of vitamins A and C. A ripe cantaloupe should have a sweet and fruity, but not overpowering aroma. The melon should yield slightly when pushed at the bottom end. The netting on the beige skin should be well-raised. Store unripe melons at room temperature, but refrigerate ripe fruit and any leftovers.

Carrots and Parsnips

Carrots are crunchy when raw and sweet when cooked. For soups, use full-size medium carrots, rather than baby carrots. Carrots can be refrigerated for 2 to 3 weeks. Avoid carrots that have a green tinge at the top, which indicates bitterness, and those that are cracked, which means they're old.

For those of you unaccustomed to parsnips, they are a long cream-colored root that resembles a carrot. They should not be eaten raw, but cooked. If the parsnips are large, the center of the stem may get woody, and it's best to cut out any tough core. They have a refrigerator life of 1 to 2 weeks.

Souper Clue

Sometimes carrots and parsnips need to be scrubbed with a brush to remove dirt. Once clean, peel with a vegetable peeler.

Both of these root vegetables can be purchased in bags or in bundles with their leaves attached. To me, it is always preferable to buy them with the tops attached, although you should cut off the tops and discard them before storing the veggies in your vegetable crisper.

Celery

Celery should be crisp and firm with leaves that show no signs of wilting. Some varieties are bright green, others are a paler color. Pascal celery is the common green type that you may see advertised in grocery circulars. Ideally, celery should last about 2 weeks in the refrigerator; however, I find it often lasts less than that. If it's beginning to lose its firmness, it can still be used in soups, but don't use it if it's completely flexible.

Souper Clue

It's a good idea to peel the fibrous strings on large celery stalks with a vegetable peeler.

Corn

Unless it's in season locally, I generally pass up so-called fresh corn. When fresh, it's the one vegetable I almost always insist on buying from a farmers' market or roadside

Souper Saver

The sugar in corn turns to starch quickly. To keep it sweet, refrigerate it immediately after you buy it and ideally cook it the same day. Husk the corn and remove the corn silk shortly before you're ready to cook it.

stand. For the recipes in this book, it doesn't matter whether you choose white, yellow, or mixed yellow and white kernels. When you buy fresh corn, check for tight husks, corn silk that is toast-colored at the top and tightly packed, and medium-size kernels. And, of course, check for the dreaded wormholes. Do not buy prepacked sets of ears with the ends cut off or those that are partially husked—all the sweet, fresh flavor will be lost.

Frozen corn is also fine for any of the soup recipes and is preferable to starchy or old, so-called "fresh" corn. In a pinch you can also use canned corn kernels that have been drained.

Cucumber

There are three types of cucumbers: waxy, English, and Kirby. Waxy cucumbers are of medium size and contain many seeds. English are long and narrow, usually covered in plastic, and have relatively few seeds. Both can be used in soups, as recipes indicate. The small Kirby cucumbers are for pickles and are generally not suitable for cooking. Cucumbers, when refrigerated, keep for about a week.

Eggplant

Eggplant comes in familiar purple and less-known white, and either can be used for soup. Slender, purple Asian eggplant is also an option. Make sure whatever eggplant you buy has a shiny skin and is firm to the touch with no soft spots. It should last about a week in the refrigerator.

Greens: Swiss Chard, Spinach, Escarole, and Romaine

Look for leaves that are brightly colored without any discolored spots or wilted edges. These greens can be very dirty and need to be washed well in a sink full of cold water, most often more than once. I usually wash them several times just to be sure, because gritty greens will spoil any soup. If you're using them for something other than soup, they should be spun dry in a salad spinner to keep them crisp.

Leeks

Leeks are a member of the onion family with a milder, somewhat sweeter taste. They resemble large scallions and should be stored in the refrigerator. Try to choose leeks that are of similar size, which is sometimes a challenge, as many markets randomly bundle them. The white part should be firm to the touch and the greens should not be yellowed.

➤ **How to cut leeks:** Slice off and discard the top green part as well as the root end. Peel and discard any tough outer layers. For slices, cut the leek in half lengthwise, then slice crosswise into half-moons. For thin strips, cut the leek lengthwise, then into 2-inch pieces, and cut into thin strips.

Souper Clue

Store cleaned, dried greens in a perforated plastic bag in the vegetable drawer of your refrigerator.

Souper Saver

Leeks can be quite gritty. Dirt is often hidden and trapped between the layers. Cut the leeks first, and then wash them.

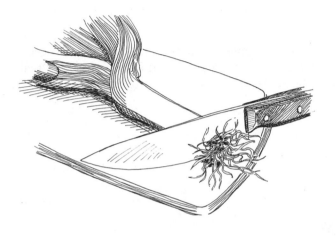

➤ **How to wash leeks:** Swish sliced leeks in a bowl of cold water. Let them stand for a minute or two so the dirt sinks to the bottom. Lift them out with a slotted spoon, skimmer, or small sieve. You'll probably have to wash them more than once.

Mushrooms

Fresh mushrooms are very perishable and should be used within a few days of purchase. Buy those that are firm, without discolored spots or a slimy surface. Always store them in the refrigerator.

Many varieties of mushrooms are now available in supermarkets and greengrocers. Wild mushrooms have more character than their white counterpart, and any dried mushrooms have an even more intense flavor. See the following page for a list to help you know what to buy:

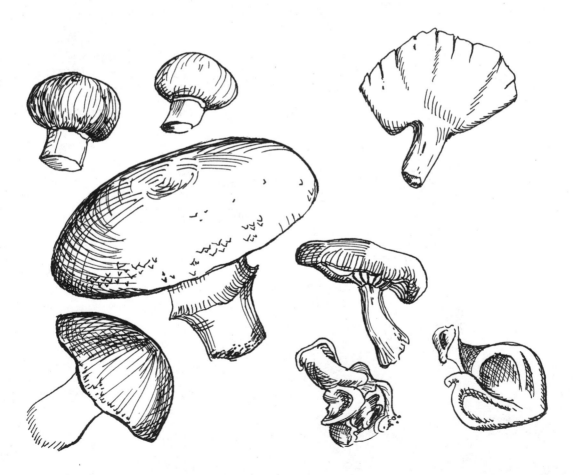

➤ **White cultivated:** These mushrooms, sometimes called button mushrooms, are the common, everyday mushrooms you find on supermarket shelves. Although mild in flavor, they are terrific in soup. Add a few wild mushrooms to them if you want a fuller mushroom taste.

➤ **Cremini:** A tan to light-brown mushroom with a slightly stronger taste than ordinary white mushrooms.

➤ **Shiitake:** Now commercially grown, these Japanese mushrooms have a marvelous rich flavor. They're terrific in any mushroom dish, particularly soups. Do not use the stems because they impart an unpleasant taste. Twist the stems off the caps and discard them, then slice the caps into strips. Shiitakes are also available dried and should be reconstituted before using, and the stems discarded.

➤ **Porcini or Cepes:** Highly flavorful, these wild mushrooms, native to Italy and France as well as parts of North America, can be combined with white or cremini mushrooms in soups. They're often used dried and reconstituted. Although they may seem costly, they're worth it—a little goes a long way in terms of taste.

➤ **Chanterelles:** Another species of wild mushrooms, chanterelles have a delicate taste and can be combined with other varieties in mushroom soups. They are also available dried.

➤ **Portabello:** Large and meaty, these mushrooms are best for grilling or sautéing, although you can add a chopped one to any mushroom soup.

➤ **Wood and Cloud Ear:** These dried Chinese mushrooms have a unique, earthy taste and must be reconstituted.

Souper Clue

To clean mushrooms, wipe the stems with a damp cloth or paper towel. If the mushrooms are very dirty, swirl them quickly and gently in a sink filled with cool water and drain them immediately so their flavor won't be lost.

Souper Clue

Instead of chopping reconstituted mushrooms, cut them into small pieces with scissors. It's easier and just as effective.

➤ **Morels:** These are a 4-star mushroom, incredibly tasty with an intense flavor. They should be reserved for sauces or sautéed with vegetables such as asparagus. I wouldn't use them in soup.

➤ **Oyster:** These white, irregularly shaped mushrooms have a very delicate taste. They can be combined with other mushrooms in soups and stirfries. If dried, they should be reconstituted.

Generally 4 to 6 dried mushrooms will be adequate for boosting mushroom taste in soups. They must be reconstituted before you use them. Put the mushrooms in a small bowl and pour boiling water over them. Let them stand for 20 to 30 minutes. With a slotted spoon remove the mushrooms and chop them.

Pour the mushroom-soaking liquid through a sieve lined with a paper coffee filter to remove any grit. Use the mushroom-soaking liquid in place of some of the broth. It will add a stronger mushroom flavor to the soup.

Onions

Onions, unlike their relatives, scallions and leeks, do not need to be refrigerated, but can be stored in a cool, dry place. I keep them in a wire basket so that air circulates around them. Although there are many kinds of onions—red onions, white onions, small pearl onions, sweet Walla-Walla, and Vidalia as well as large Spanish and Bermuda onions—the common yellow onion of medium size is preferable for soups unless another type is specified.

Souper Saver

Buying in bulk can save money. If one of the onions is going bad, discard it immediately. One bad onion can spoil the lot.

Choose onions that are firm to the touch and covered with papery yellow skin. Avoid onions that have soft spots or a strong odor as they may be beginning to spoil.

Peas: Garden or English, Snow Peas, and Sugar Snap Peas

Souper Idea

Substitute fresh sugar snap peas, which are sweeter, for snow peas in the soup recipes if you want. When in season, they are less expensive.

Garden or English peas are the everyday sweet, round, green peas that we eat shelled, the ones that invariably roll off your fork onto your lap. Frozen common peas are just fine in any soup recipe, but never use canned, which are mushy and comparatively flavorless. Snow peas and sugar snap peas are relatives, but the entire pod of both of these can be eaten. Remove the thin string that runs along the bottom of the pod before preparing them. Pods for any peas should be bright green and crisp. Peas will keep, refrigerated, for about 3 days, although you are losing more of the fresh sweet flavor every day.

Potatoes

Although there are endless varieties, from purple to gold, there are only two main categories of potatoes: waxy or starchy. Waxy or all-purpose are the best kind for soup. These include Maine, Long Island, round red or white, and long white potatoes. The second category, starchy potatoes, include Idaho and russet. Although excellent for baking, starchy potatoes will fall apart in soup. New potatoes aren't a type of potato, but are simply potatoes that were harvested young and should be cooked soon after purchase.

Potatoes should be firm and without blemishes, cracks, or sprouts. You may need to scrub them with a brush to remove any dirt. Store in a cool, dry place for up to 1 month, but don't refrigerate them. I keep mine in a bin or basket so the air circulates freely around them.

Radishes

Most folks are familiar with the small, round, red radish, which is often used in salads. Daikon, a variety popular in Japan, is white and quite large. It is sometimes sold in pieces. Purchase firm radishes and store them in the refrigerator for about a week.

Scallions

Most scallions, also known as spring onions or green onions, are young onions, although occasionally they can be immature leeks. They should be kept refrigerated. Select scallions with a firm white end and bright green tops.

> ➤ **How to cut a scallion:** trim a couple inches from the greens, even if you're going to use these for garnish, and cut off the root end. With the tip of a paring knife, loosen and peel any tough outer layers.

> ➤ **If you're using only the white part:** trim to just where the stem begins to turn bright green. Slice into thin pieces or chunks as called for in the recipe.

Squash

There are two types of squash, winter and summer. Winter squashes include butternut, Hubbard, acorn, spaghetti squash, and pumpkin. Summer squashes include zucchini and crookneck, also known as yellow squash. All except spaghetti squash make terrific soup.

Winter squash can be kept unrefrigerated in a cool, dry place for several months. The tough outer skin must be peeled before steaming or boiling the squash, but should be left intact if you are baking it. One way to prepare winter squash for soup or a side dish is to peel it, cut it in half lengthwise and scoop out the seeds, then cut it into evenly sized cubes, about $1^1/_2$ to 2 inches. The squash is ready to be cooked until it's tender either by steaming, simmering, or microwaving. Once cooked, it can then be pureed. Another method is to slice it in half lengthwise, take out the seeds, and place it skin-side up in a glass baking dish. Bake in a 350°F oven or microwave it until very tender. Scoop out the soft pulp and puree.

Summer squash should be firm to the touch. In soups, it can be sliced, diced, or cut into half-moons or thin strips. It requires no peeling and can last about 4 to 5 days in the refrigerator.

Sweet Potatoes

Sweet potatoes are beautiful pale orange-fleshed potatoes with a delightfully sweet taste. Try to only buy what you will use, as they don't keep for too long—only a couple of weeks if kept in a cool, dry, and dark place. Don't refrigerate them or their deliciously mealy texture changes. Be adventurous and substitute sweet potatoes occasionally for regular potatoes in the soup recipes.

Souper Bowl Fact

In the United States, sweet potatoes are sometimes called yams, but this is a misnomer. Real yams aren't kin to sweet potatoes.

Tomatoes

There are two types of tomatoes: plum tomatoes that have an oval or teardrop shape, and round tomatoes. Plum tomatoes are sweeter and meatier. Round tomatoes come in several sizes, from cherry to beefsteak, and also are available in a range of colors from red to pink to yellow. Tomatoes have the best flavor when left at room temperature; however, if you plan to keep ripe ones more than a few days, they can be refrigerated for a day or two to prevent them from ripening further. Fresh tomatoes can be kept at room temperature for 3 to 5 days.

For the soup recipes, choose firm, ripe, red tomatoes, either plum or round and medium in size. In winter, plum tomatoes often have superior taste to round, unless you buy those that are imported from Holland or Israel, or hydroponically grown. These are always more expensive.

Canned tomatoes are preferable to pithy, unripe tomatoes. They are economical, convenient, and work well in most of the soup recipes. They're already peeled and you don't need to seed them.

➤ **How to peel a tomato:** In a saucepan, bring water to a boil. With a paring knife, lightly cut an X in the skin on the bottom of a whole tomato without piercing its flesh. Immerse the tomatoes in the boiling water for 15 to 30 seconds. With a slotted spoon or sieve, remove the tomatoes and set them aside. If the phone rang or by mistake you left the tomatoes a little longer in the boiling water, plunge them into a bowl of ice water to stop the cooking. Peel the skin off with the tip of the paring knife. It should slip right off.

Souper Clue

If recipes call for peeled, seeded tomatoes, peel them first, then seed them, reserving the juice if you want to add it to the soup.

➤ **How to seed a tomato:** Slice the tomato lengthwise from top to bottom, and cut out the core at the top. Flick the seeds out with your finger. If you want to reserve the juice, before removing the seeds squeeze the tomato gently over a sieve set in a bowl, then flick out the seeds with your finger.

Turnips and Rutabagas

Turnips are round or oval white-fleshed roots with a purple tinged top. Their larger relatives, rutabagas (also known as Swedish turnips or Swedes), have yellow flesh with similar purple markings and are sometimes coated with wax. Both need to be washed and peeled. Use them interchangeably.

The Least You Need to Know

➤ Select firm vegetables with a smooth, unblemished skin.

➤ Only buy in bulk the vegetables that you use often.

➤ Vegetables that are in season are cheaper and taste best.

➤ Frozen vegetables are good for soups when fresh are too expensive or out of season. If you don't have fresh vegetables, frozen are nearly always preferable to canned.

Chapter 5

From the Dairy Case

In This Chapter

➤ Butter versus margarine

➤ The difference between cream, milk, buttermilk, yogurt, and sour cream

➤ Which cheeses are right for soup?

➤ The types of tofu and their uses

Many dairy products are used in soup to lend creaminess, to balance other ingredients, and to improve texture as well as to add a final accent or garnish. It's not necessary for most people to completely shy away from dairy products, but to learn to use them in moderation. Used in small quantities, milk, cream, sour cream, cheese, and butter provide essential calcium and fats. Two-percent milk, low-fat buttermilk, nonfat yogurt, and low-fat or nonfat sour cream offer the same nutritional benefits with sometimes significantly less fat than the original versions.

Butter and Margarine

I use butter in some recipes because of its delicately rich and unbeatable flavor. Butter comes in sticks or tubs and is labeled either salted or sweet, which means unsalted. I prefer sweet because its taste is purer and creamier, but use whichever you like. Butter lasts for 2 to 3 weeks in the refrigerator. You can buy it when it's on sale and freeze it. It can be frozen for up to a year.

Margarine, although it looks like butter, lacks its unique, characteristic flavor, and you do compromise taste by substituting it. Feel free to use margarine, however, if that's what you prefer. Margarine is not any healthier than butter—it's a hydrogenated fat, which some experts now believe actually raises cholesterol levels. Stick margarine has the same fat and calorie count as butter. Reduced-fat margarine has some caloric advantage.

Souper Bowl Fact

Measuring butter and margarine out of a tub can be tricky to do. Use butter or margarine in sticks instead of out of a tub, because it's much easier to measure.

$^1/_4$ pound = 1 stick

1 stick = $^1/_2$ cup or 8 tablespoons

$^1/_2$ stick = 4 tablespoons

$^1/_4$ stick = 2 tablespoons

$^1/_8$ stick = 1 tablespoon

Cream, Half-and-Half, Milk, and Buttermilk

Some soup recipes call for these items interchangeably. The choice is yours, according to how creamy a texture or how rich a flavor you want the end product to have. Store them all in the refrigerator in sealed containers.

When choosing cream, use light cream, which usually has 20 percent fat. Heavy cream is used for whipping and contains nearly double the amount of fat. Half-and-half has 10 to 12 percent fat.

Whole milk has approximately 3 to 4 percent fat. Two-percent milk is half that.

Old-fashioned and homemade buttermilk were the by-products from making butter. Today, commercial buttermilk is produced by adding a bacterial culture to skim or low-fat milk to create the texture and flavor of the original. Most labels indicate this with the words "cultured buttermilk." It has a distinctively tart and tangy taste and should be used only in recipes where it's called for.

Souper Bowl Fact

Make your own preservative-free half-and-half by combining equal parts of milk and light cream. It is purer and fresher, but it won't last as long as commercially made half-and-half products that generally contain additives to lengthen their shelf life.

Souper Bowl Fact

Most dairy products are marked with a "use by" date indicating their shelf life.

Yogurt

Yogurt is made from milk that is fermented by adding a bacteria or culture. It is then incubated until it is thickened, creamy, and slightly acidic. Yogurt can be made from whole, low-fat, skim, or fat-free milk, and all these types of yogurt are on the market.

In the soup recipes, use plain yogurt. It is generally packaged in eight-ounce to one-quart containers. My preference is lowfat. Fat-free yogurt has a thinner consistency than low-fat or whole-milk versions, and is not as pleasing to the palate in soup. Generally yogurt will last in the fridge for about one week after its expiration date.

Souper Bowl Fact

Yogurt with active cultures has long been believed to be beneficial to health and an aid to the digestive process.

Sour Cream

Sour cream is a cultured milk product with a thick, creamy texture and a delightfully tart taste, but unlike yogurt it has not been fermented. Instead it has been chilled and aged for 1 to 2 days. There are several types on the market—whole milk, low-fat, and nonfat—all of which are excellent choices for any recipe. They can be used interchangeably.

Tofu or Bean Curd

Found in the dairy or produce case of many markets, tofu or bean curd is made from curdled soy milk that is pressed into a cake. It is an excellent source of protein and calcium, low in calories, and cholesterol free. The only drawback is its somewhat high sodium content. It has a satiny texture that is velvety smooth. Tofu itself is bland and rather tasteless, but it absorbs the flavor of whatever food it's added to. It comes in firm and soft varieties as well as silken varieties. If it's to be cubed in soup, it's best to use firm tofu that can be cubed easily and will not fall apart once it's added to simmering broth.

Souper Idea

Silken tofu is not pressed, but coagulated, and is sold in boxes. Puree it in a blender, and it will have a consistency similar to yogurt. It can be used in cream soups instead of cream or half-and-half, but must be stirred very well before it's added. It won't add to or detract from any taste already in the soup.

You'll sometimes find tofu sold in open tubs that are filled with water. To avoid any possible contamination, it's advisable to purchase it in sealed containers. Most tofu packages are dated. If the package has no date, it should keep, unopened, for 4 to 5 days after purchase. If you have some left over from a recipe, keep it for about 3 days submerged in a container of cold water, but remember to change the water daily. Always store fresh and opened, boxed tofu in the refrigerator.

Cheese

Cheeses are marvelous flavorful additions to creamy and pureed vegetable soups as well as tasty garnishes for many heartier vegetable soups. Here are a few that are used in the recipes.

➤ **Cheddar:** Whether domestic or imported from its native England, this highly popular, firm cheese can be purchased in a range of tastes from mild to sharp to very sharp, depending on how long it's aged. The longer it has been aged, the stronger its taste. Once opened, keep it in the refrigerator wrapped in plastic wrap. To use it in soups, grate it on the largest side of a four-sided grater or in your food processor fitted with the shredding disk.

➤ **Parmesan and Romano:** Both Parmesan and Romano, hard cheeses that have been aged for at least 2 and up to 7 years, originally hail from Italy. Parmigiano Reggiano is Italy's superior Parmesan with a complex flavor and granular texture. There are several varieties of Romano cheese, one of the more famous being Pecorino Romano, which technically should be made from sheep's milk.

It's fine to buy domestic Parmesan or Romano for soups, and there are several good producers. For superior taste, try to buy wedges and grate the cheese yourself on a small-holed cheese grater, or cut it into pieces and pulse it in a food processor fitted with the metal blade. Avoid canned or bottled Parmesan, which has little resemblance to the real thing. Store any extra grated cheese in the refrigerator.

Souper Clue

It's best to buy cheeses and grate them yourself, but that's not always possible when you're in a hurry. Some stores grate their own and package it, and you can usually buy packages of commercially grated and packaged cheese in the dairy section of the supermarket.

➤ **Blue:** Blue cheese, with characteristic greenish-blue veins formed by mold, is known for its distinctively strong aroma and taste. Many countries have their own versions, although most styles are also made domestically. Examples of the more noted blues are French Roquefort, English Stilton, Italian Gorgonzola, Danish Danablu and American Maytag. To use it in soups and salads, crumble it gently with your fingertips.

➤ **Swiss Cheese:** A favorite among domestic cheeses, this firm, pale yellow cheese with large holes has a mildly nutty flavor. It imitates the popular imported Swiss Gruyère and Emmenthaler. Because Swiss cheese melts smoothly and doesn't become stringy, it is ideal for French Onion Soup. It either can be thinly sliced or grated. Use the largest side of a four-sided grater or grate it in a food processor fitted with the shredding disk.

Souper Clue

To keep cheese fresh, wrap wedges and slices in plastic wrap and put grated cheese in an airtight container, and refrigerate.

The Least You Need to Know

➤ Dairy products are a good source of calcium.

➤ Dairy products add a creamy texture to soup.

➤ Sour cream, yogurt, and grated cheese are great garnishes.

➤ For the best flavor, buy cheese in chunks or slabs and grate it yourself.

Chapter 6

From the Butcher and Fishmonger

In This Chapter

➤ Learn which cuts of meat are suitable for soup.

➤ Find out which chicken parts make the tastiest soup.

➤ Get tips on buying fresh or frozen seafood.

Meat, poultry, or seafood are the mainstay of a multitude of dishes including soups, adding their individual character and depth of flavor. These versatile ingredients, the basis of delicious broth, act as the predominant component in several hearty soups and chowders as well as agreeable accents in lighter fare.

As with any fresh food item, the quality of the ingredients affects the quality of the finished dish. Always purchase meat, poultry, or seafood from a reputable store—a good supermarket, butcher, or fish shop. When buying from a butcher or fish shop, ask how long the product will last in your refrigerator.

When buying prepackaged items, check the sell-by date on the label. It's best to use it by that day or freeze it. Often you'll find that today's bargain or what's on sale must be used right away or frozen. If you decide to freeze meat, poultry, or seafood, take it out of the store's packaging—never just toss it in the freezer. Rewrap it in plastic wrap, then in foil or freezer wrap or a self-sealing plastic bag to protect it from freezer burn. Label and date it so you know how long it's been in your freezer, and use it within two months.

Meat

The meat used in soups is generally the same cut used in stews, because both dishes tend to simmer slowly for an hour or two until the meat is tender. Meat should be well marbled and yes, that means there should be some strands of fat running through it; otherwise, the meat will become tough and stringy. Trim visible excess fat from the outer edges. Whether you're making a beef or lamb soup, pass up packages labeled "stew or soup meat." Often they're of low quality and include scraps that can be quite fatty. Instead, look for a specific cut that is cubed or buy a whole piece of meat and cube it yourself.

The Right Cuts

➤ **Beef:** chuck or bottom round, cubed; leaner top round, cubed; and if you don't mind bones, short ribs, cut into 3-inch pieces

➤ **Oxtail:** cut between the joints into pieces

➤ **Lamb:** shoulder, cubed

Souper Saver

When handling fresh meat, poultry, and seafood, hygiene is important. To prevent bacterial contamination, after use, wash cutting boards and utensils in hot, soapy water, then rinse well. And don't forget to wash countertops and hands as well.

Poultry

Years ago, stewing hens, also called fowl, were readily available. These tougher birds made wonderful broth, soup, and stews, but now they're very hard to find. The meat from chicken thighs has more flavor than that of chicken breasts. It takes a little longer to cook, but is wonderful in soups.

The Right Cuts

➤ **Best for broth only:** chicken or turkey parts such as thighs, legs, backs, necks, and wings, or a meaty turkey carcass, cut up

➤ **Best for broth and soup meat:** whole chicken, cut up, or flavorful parts such as thighs or legs from chicken or turkey

➤ **Best meat to add to soup, cooked or raw, cubed or cut into strips as the recipe indicates:** boneless chicken breasts or thighs; meat from turkey thighs; leftover chicken; leftover turkey breast or thighs

Wash whole chickens and chicken parts with cold water before using them, and pat dry with a paper towel. If there are bits of the innards or blood left on the chicken, scrub it gently with coarse or kosher salt and rinse well.

Seafood

Poor seafood can ruin any dish, so always buy the best quality, freshest fish or shellfish you can from a reliable market that keeps their fish on ice or in a refrigerated case. Fishmongers with high turnover often have the freshest product, which directly translates into the best-tasting. Neither the market nor the seafood should have an offensively strong smell. Because large fisheries now flash-freeze products, those products are often preferable to fresh seafood of questionable quality.

Souper Saver

To minimize any potential health hazards, defrost poultry and meat overnight in the refrigerator.

Fish fillets and scallops should be firm to the touch and have no bruises or brown spots that might indicate spoilage. Whole fish should have gills that are moist and red or bright pink, eyes that are clear and bulging, not milky or sunken, as well as bright and shiny scales. The shells of clams and mussels should be closed. Shrimp should not have yellowed or blackened shells. Fresh crabmeat should be dated (or ask the fishmonger how long it will last). Frozen products should have no signs of freezer burn, such as excessive ice crystals, or be dried out or chalky looking. If buying canned products, make sure the can isn't rusty or dented.

clams

➤ **Using frozen fish:** Frozen fish should thaw at room temperature for about half an hour, then be cooked. The partially frozen fish will remain moister and more tender in whatever dish you're using it in than if you let it thaw completely. Because the fish will still be partially frozen, you'll need to increase the cooking time by one third to one half. For example, if the fresh or fully thawed fish is to cook for 10 minutes, you'll need to cook it for it for 12 to 15 minutes.

➤ **Using fresh clams:** For the soup recipes, use hard-shell clams or quahogs. Wash the clams well with a wire brush. Let the clams sit in a sink or basin filled with cold water for 20 to 30 minutes so they spit out any sand or grit. Don't let them stand longer or they'll die, which will make them inedible.

To cook clams, bring 1^1/$_2$ cups water to a boil in a large Dutch oven or pot. Add the clams and reduce the heat to medium-low. Cover and simmer for 5 minutes or until the clams are opened. Remove the clams with a slotted spoon and discard any that did not open. Strain the cooking liquid and reserve to use as broth. For the chowder recipes, remove the clams from their shells and set aside.

➤ **Using fresh mussels:** Wash the mussels well with a wire brush. Fill a basin or the sink with cold water and add a couple of generous pinches of flour or cornmeal. Let the mussels soak in this water for 30 to 60 minutes, no longer, or they'll die and you'll have to discard them instead of eating them. Rinse well. Pull or cut off the beard, the tough threads that the mussel uses to attach itself to rocks.

mussel

To cook mussels, bring 1^1/$_2$ cups water or ^{3}/$_4$ cup water and ^{3}/$_4$ cup white wine to a boil in a large pot. Add the mussels and reduce the heat to medium-low. Cover and simmer for 5 minutes or until the mussels are opened. Remove the mussels with a slotted spoon and discard any that did not open. Strain the cooking liquid and reserve to use as part of the broth. For the soup recipe, remove the mussels from their shells and set aside.

➤ **To devein shrimp:** Peel the shrimp. With a sharp paring knife, make a shallow slit along the back of the shrimp. With the tip of the knife, loosen, remove, and discard the dark vein.

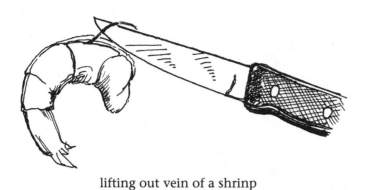

lifting out vein of a shrinp

Souper Clue

Sometimes certain fish might not be available, but that doesn't mean you can't make a recipe. Ask the fishmonger to recommend a good substitute.

The Least You Need to Know

➤ Marbled cuts such as beef chuck and lamb shoulder are ideal because they become quite tender.

➤ Use flavorful dark-meat chicken parts such as thighs and backs for soup.

➤ Fish shouldn't have a strong odor. Get to know a good fishmonger and buy the best quality.

➤ Cook only live shellfish with tightly closed shells, and discard any shellfish that don't open when cooked.

Chapter 7

Season It

In This Chapter

➤ Using and storing dried spices and herbs

➤ Fresh versus dried—which herbs to use and why

➤ Making the most of garlic, ginger, chilies, and other seasonings

---

As we widen our culinary horizons to take advantage of tastes from around the world, today's food is bursting with flavor. Present-day cooks have a broader culinary repertoire, encompassing family favorites as well as regional specialties. The popularity of a wide range of ethnic dishes has transformed formerly exotic seasonings, such as allspice, cumin, fresh basil, fresh cilantro, and sesame oil, into everyday items that are available in most supermarkets.

Learning how to season correctly is an art that requires knowledge, patience, and the courage to indulge in a bit of experimentation. Here are a few helpful hints:

➤ When using a new herb or spice, get familiar with it—smell it and taste it on the tip of your tongue.

➤ Start with the amount a recipe calls for—flavors can concentrate during the cooking process and easily overpower a dish. If you want to add more next time, make any increases in small increments.

➤ Always salt soup or broth near or at the end of the cooking time.

➤ Spices should be added toward the beginning of the cooking process.

➤ Herbs can be added in the beginning and during the cooking time. Some herbs are stirred in right before serving.

➤ When garnishing with herbs, always use fresh.

Souper Bowl Fact

Although most spices originally come from Asia and the Indonesian Spice Islands, the East doesn't have a monopoly. Some are now grown elsewhere—ginger in Jamaica and Nigeria, cloves in Zanzibar and Madagascar, and nutmeg in Grenada. Hot chilies, a popular spice native to the Americas, made their way around the globe, and are used from Mexico to Asia, either fresh or dried and ground.

Spices

Highly valued throughout the ages for their culinary and medicinal properties, spices are aromatic seasonings—the seeds, roots, fruits, flowers, or bark of a variety of tropical trees and plants. This prized commodity used in food, perfume, medicine, ceremonies, and religious rites could buy freedom for a medieval serf. Spices sparked Columbus's search for an alternate route to the East Indies and his subsequent westward voyage to America. Except for fresh ginger, chilies, and lemon grass, they are always used dried. Spices can be found in markets either whole or ground.

Buying Spices

Ground spices have a six-month shelf life after they're opened before their potency diminishes dramatically. It's best to buy them as you need them and in small quantities. If you use a particular spice often, then by all means go ahead and buy a larger amount; otherwise, buy small amounts and replenish periodically. Whole spices will last longer, up to a year or more, and you can grind them yourself.

Toasting and Grinding Spices

Some whole spices such as cumin, coriander, and fennel seeds benefit from light toasting before grinding. This process releases more of the natural aroma, oils, and flavor. Grind whole spices, with or without toasting first, in a mini food processor or small spice or coffee mill that you use for that purpose. Try to grind them as you need them, but know that you can store home-ground spices in a sealed jar. Unless you're very experienced and can tell them apart by color and smell, make sure you label the container.

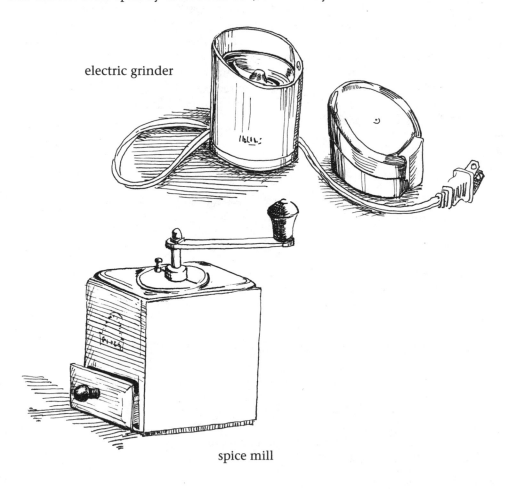

electric grinder

spice mill

Souper Clue

To toast spices, heat them in a dry skillet over medium heat until slightly browned and fragrant, just a few moments. Toss them or stir them occasionally while they're in the pan so they don't burn, and remove them from the hot pan as soon as they're done. Burned spices have an unpleasant taste and must be thrown out.

Storing Spices

Keep spices in a sealed glass or plastic container in a cool, dark place, away from heat, preferably not above the stove or the oven. Make sure you store them on their own or with canned goods. Some foods, such as chocolate and rice, absorb the flavor of the spices—and who wants to munch on curried chocolate?

Superstar Seasonings

Salt

Salt is used more often and in more foods than any other ingredient, and it doubles as both a flavoring agent and a preservative. Treasured throughout history for its amazing properties, salt marries the individual elements in a dish. Food without salt often seems to be lacking the proverbial "something." Even a small amount blends and unifies tastes in a dish that otherwise seems unfinished. The only trick is to use it sparingly. Start by adding a small amount, stir well, then taste, and carefully add more if you want. In the soup recipes, begin with $1/2$ teaspoon. If you want to be more cautious or have used a salty commercial broth, taste first, and if you need to season, start with $1/4$ teaspoon.

Souper Bowl Fact

Kosher salt has a medium grain and is the top choice of many chefs for cooking. **Sea salt** comes in medium and fine grain and can be used like common table salt, and either is excellent for general cooking. When baking, always use common table salt because it's finely ground.

Pepper

Pepper is one of world's most popular seasonings, adding an aromatic sharpness to food. Black pepper is the most common, and several varieties are available: bold-flavored tellichery, pungent and hot Brazilian, and smooth and balanced Malabar. When you buy whole peppercorns, the type is often listed on the label. Other kinds of pepper used in cooking include the milder white pepper and mixed peppercorn blends of white, black, pink, and green.

Ground pepper loses its character within a couple of months, so it's wise to buy it whole. Make sure you also buy a peppermill for black peppercorns so you can grind it fresh. If you want to grind different varieties regularly, it's more convenient to have a separate mill for each kind than to empty a mill and get rid of the pepper residue each time you want to change the peppercorns. Sometimes one type of pepper isn't completely out of the mechanism when you grind another kind.

Cameo Roles

They're small but they're vital. Garlic, ginger, chilies, and lemon grass are sold fresh in the produce section of your market. They are the primary flavor underpinning many cuisines and are used extensively in soup.

Garlic

Garlic, a cousin of onions and leeks, is sold in whole heads composed of separate cloves. Store it in a cool, dark, dry place, away from other food. I generally keep mine with onions.

Heads should keep for a month or two, whereas individual cloves will stay fresh for about two weeks. Discard any shriveled, discolored, or sprouting cloves.

Cloves can be of varying sizes, from plump to small, depending on whether they're from the exterior or inner core. When a recipe calls for a clove of garlic, it refers to a plump one. You may need to use two to three of the small ones to get the equivalent amount. Bottled, chopped garlic and peeled whole cloves are available in many refrigerator cases in markets and should be stored in the fridge at home. Always use fresh as the dried is a poor alternative, lacking its pungent character.

Most often garlic is added to onions or other aromatic vegetables that have already been softened. When cooking garlic, make sure there's enough oil, cook over medium-low to medium heat, and stir frequently. You must take care that the garlic doesn't burn because it will acquire an unpleasantly acrid taste that can ruin an entire dish. If it burns, you'll have to discard the lot, not only the garlic but also the veggies it was cooked with, and start afresh.

Souper Clue

To peel cloves easily, put the flat side of a kitchen knife on the clove and tap the knife gently but firmly. The skin should break and peel easily. Be careful not to smash the garlic, which makes it more prone to burning.

Ginger

Always use fresh ginger in the soups. Dried ginger has a different taste and is not a substitute in

Souper Bowl Fact

Here are some measurement equivalents:

1 plump clove garlic = $^1/_2$ teaspoon minced, fresh garlic

1-inch piece ginger = 1 tablespoon minced, fresh ginger

cooking, although it is wonderful for many baked goods. Buy ginger that has a strong fragrance and is firm, with smooth, unwrinkled skin. Unpeeled, it should last for 2 to 3 weeks in the refrigerator. Remember to peel the ginger before grating or mincing it.

Fresh Chilies

Numerous types of fresh chilies can be found in most produce sections. Although I frequently use jalapeños, cayenne, or serranos, use those that you prefer. Whether fresh or dried, chilies need to be handled carefully because they can burn your skin, eyes, and mouth.

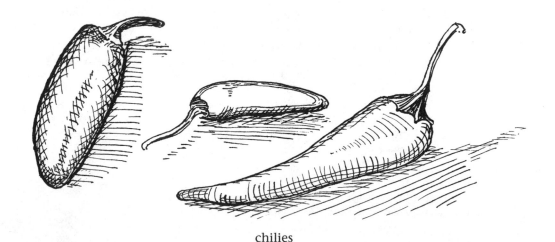

chilies

How hot a chili is, even within a particular type, can and does vary. Some jalapeños are very hot and others are relatively mild. You might want to taste a tiny sliver to decide how much you want to use before you add it to a dish. To reduce the heat a bit,

Souper Bowl Fact

Always wash your hands well after touching the chilies or their seeds. Keep your fingers away from your face and eyes. For extra protection, wear thin rubber or latex gloves to prevent skin irritation when handling chilies.

remove the ribs as well as the seeds from the chili. In many recipes, a quantity range is given, such as 1 to 2 jalapeños, taking into account their fluctuating "heat" factor. If you prefer a hint of chili, use less than the recipes call for. You know what to do if you want it hotter.

Lemon Grass and Lime Leaves

Native to Southeast Asia and central to Thai and Vietnamese cuisine, lemon grass and lime leaves can be purchased in Asian groceries and in the ethnic sections of supermarkets and specialty stores.

Lemon-grass stalks are available fresh or dried. Fresh is preferable, but one stalk is roughly equivalent to $1^1/_2$ to 2 tablespoons dried and chopped. Because the dried is less potent, the exchange ratio is not equal.

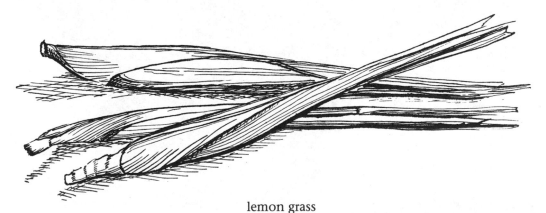

lemon grass

Thai lime leaves, also called kaffir lime leaves, are from the makrud tree. They are available either fresh or dried. If you use dried, their flavor is less intense, and you might want to use an extra leaf or two.

Herbs

Herbs bring another dimension to food, subtly enhancing its flavor and graciously garnishing its appearance. Like spices, herbs have historically been used in cooking, medicines, and rituals. Although widely marketed in dried form, herbs, the leafy part of plants and trees, are increasingly available fresh in produce aisles. Many people use dried as a matter of convenience, but some herbs should always be used fresh as their distinctive aroma and taste are completely lost when dried. These include the everyday favorites of parsley and flat-leaf parsley, cilantro, dill, and mint as well as the less commonplace chervil and sage. Basil in particular should only be used fresh, as dried basil barely even resembles the fresh in flavor. Dried herbs have a longer shelf life than fresh, about 6 to 8 months for commercially dried and up to a year for home-dried.

Storing Fresh Herbs

Keep fresh herbs in the refrigerator because they are highly perishable, but remove any decaying leaves before storing. Wrap them gently in a lightly dampened but not wet paper towel. If the leaves are too wet, they will spoil quickly. Put the bundle in a plastic bag, or wrap it loosely in plastic wrap, or put it in a sealable plastic container.

Parsley, cilantro, and mint can also be stored in the refrigerator with stems down in a small cup of water. You can cover the leafy top loosely with a plastic bag.

Washing and Chopping Fresh Herbs

Before using herbs, look and taste to see whether they are dirty. Sometimes they are well washed before you buy them and are sold in sealed plastic containers. Rinse them under cold running water, shake them gently over the sink to get rid of excess water, and pat them dry with a paper towel.

Souper Clue

If you've got a green thumb, grow your own herbs in a small garden, in pots on the stoop or patio, or in window boxes. Once you've used fresh, you'll notice the difference and try to use them whenever possible.

Only use leaves that are fresh-looking. Discard any yellowed, slimy, or blemished leaves from such herbs as parsley, basil, mint, and cilantro. The stems of herbs, including parsley, should not be chopped or used; use only the leaves. Gently separate leaves from stems so they don't become bruised. The exception is cilantro, whose thin stems are occasionally chopped in Thai cuisine. Dill should not be chopped. With a pair of scissors, snip its feathery fronds from the stem into small pieces.

When herbs are to be chopped for cooking they should be minced or chopped finely. The only exceptions are when whole herbs are specifically called for, as in a bouquet garni, and for garnishes where small sprigs or whole leaves are more visually appealing accents.

Souper Bowl Fact

Traditionally, a bouquet garni is a small bunch of herbs—parsley, thyme, and bay leaf—tied together, wrapped in a piece of cheesecloth, or in the outer layer of a leek. It's added to a dish to augment its flavor. Tying the herbs together makes them easier to remove from a finished dish. Now bouquets garnis often include other herb and spice combinations.

Drying Fresh Herbs

If you have too much of a fresh herb, whether from your garden or leftover from a market purchase, you can dry the herbs so they don't go to waste. They're still "fresher," and thus tastier, than commercially dried. Rinse the herbs and pat dry. Leave cleaned herbs out to air-dry, preferably tied together in bunches and hanging upside down. They should be dry within a few days. When you're certain they are completely dry, remove the leaves from the stalks and crush. Store home-dried herbs in a covered container for up to a year.

The Least You Need to Know

➤ Buy herbs and spices as you need them, in amounts that you can use in about six months.

➤ Store spices in a cool, dry place in well-sealed containers.

➤ To bring out the flavor of spices, toast them briefly in a hot, dry skillet before using.

➤ Use fresh herbs instead of dried—especially parsley, basil, cilantro, dill, and mint—whenever possible.

Part 3
Souper Chef

When it's time to make a meal, having a workable game plan is key. You, the cook, need a strategy from start to finish. The chapters in this section give you the know-how to get from reading recipes to embarking on a sane shopping trip and back to the kitchen.

You'll learn all the processes, beginning with organizing your initial preparations—a commonsense procedure called "mise en place"—that makes the whole cooking experience more pleasurable. You'll also get the inside scoop on which techniques are commonly used in making soup, and when and where to apply them, as well as advice on how to cook and store food safely. There's even a chapter on improvising and substitutions that will give you the confidence to experiment and create some of your own chefs d'oeuvre.

Chapter 8

Ready... Set... SOUP!

In This Chapter

➤ Inventories, shopping lists, and strategies

➤ Learn about *mise en place*

➤ Prepping—what are the various cuts and measures?

You've browsed through recipes and decided which one appeals to you for which you have both the time and inclination to prepare. Here are a few pointers to guide you through the cooking process.

Getting Started

The first step is to check your own stock before heading out to shop. As obvious as this seems, it's annoying to have to make a second trip or to end up with four bottles of ground cinnamon on your shelf. Do you have a blender? Don't you have a bag of apples in the garage? Are the onions still fresh? Just how old is that curry powder hidden behind the box of salt? Should it be thrown out and replaced?

After you've finished your in-house inventory, make a shopping list. It's easiest if you group the items by category, the way you're likely to find them in the store: produce, dairy, meat, canned goods, spices, etcetera. This way you won't do as much back-tracking from aisle to aisle. Head off for grocery shopping—to a supermarket, greengrocer, butcher, or fish shop—but wherever you go, they should be a places where the quality is consistently good for a reasonable price.

Souper Preparations

Mise en Place

After shopping, read the recipe thoroughly once again so you know what you need to do. Then it's time to round up everything required to make your chosen dish. Chefs call this activity *mise en place*, a French phrase that literally means "put in place," colloquially referred to in shorthand by professional cooks as their *place*.

To begin, you'll need to gather all the equipment—pots, pans, measuring spoons and cups, blenders, sieves, skimmers, and other utensils. Keep them handy so you don't have to root through drawers and cabinets once you've started cooking, which can lead to mild panic and/or to burning food that's already in progress. In addition to equipment, you must lay out all the ingredients you'll use.

To complete your *place* you'll have to prep the ingredients, which includes any and all measuring, cutting, and precooking. After everything is ready, then and *only* then should you begin to actually make the dish. This practical process helps ensure a successful outcome whether you're making a simple soup or the most elegant pastry.

Delicate items such as seafood, poultry, and meat can be kept in the fridge until you're ready to prep them, and it's sometimes a good idea to cover them loosely and return them to the fridge if you're not going to use them within 15 to 30 minutes, so they don't have a chance to spoil.

Prep It

The way you prep an item for cooking can determine the result. Follow both the recipe instructions and these guidelines.

It's In the Cut

To make your time in the kitchen easier, familiarize yourself with the terms and the different cutting methods that are used in the recipes. Your knife should be sharp before you begin.

➤ **Chop:** To cut food into irregular pieces that are $1/4$ inch to $1/2$ inch. Vegetables such as onions, carrots, celery, and tomatoes are often chopped.

➤ **Cube:** To cut food into fairly uniform squares, from $1/2$ inch up to 2 inches, as indicated in the recipe. Meats are often cubed, as are large vegetables such as eggplant and butternut squash.

➤ **Dice:** To cut food, such as onions, into uniformly shaped pieces that are $1/4$ inch to $1/2$ inch. This is basically a smaller cube and is used primarily for vegetables, to give the finished dish a more polished look.

➤ **Mince:** To cut into small pieces of less than $1/8$ inch. It's the smallest cut and helps release flavors in aromatic foods. It is primarily used for garlic, ginger, shallots, and fresh herbs.

➤ **Shred:** To cut into relatively thin but irregular strips. This is generally done on a grater, and the side of the grater that's used determines how thick the shreds will be. Cabbage and carrots are usually done on the largest holes, whereas harder or aromatic items such as Parmesan and Romano cheese, lemon zest, or fresh ginger, are grated on smaller holes. Some food, such as lettuce, spinach, and cabbage, can also be shredded by slicing it very thin.

➤ **Slice:** To cut food into pieces of uniform thickness.

➤ **Very Thinly Slice:** To cut food into uniformly thin pieces about $1/8$-inch thick or less.

➤ **Slice in Very Thin Strips:** To cut food into uniformly thin strips or matchsticks about $1/8$-inch thick. This cut is also known as julienne or matchstick and is often used for vegetables such as cucumber, carrot, zucchini, and yellow squash.

Whether you're chopping, dicing, mincing, or slicing, cut each raw ingredient into pieces of similar size. This doesn't mean you have to measure with a ruler; your eyes are a good enough judge. If you cut one ingredient into varying sizes, each piece would have a different cooking time. During the cooking process, some would already be tender while others would still be tough.

Let's say a soup calls for sliced carrots, cubed potatoes, shredded cabbage, and beef cut into 1-inch cubes. The carrots should be basically the same length or width and the potatoes cubed to a size similar to the carrots. All the cabbage should be shredded to the same thickness. The beef should be cubed to relatively the same shape and size. This is especially important for vegetables with the same texture such as carrots, potatoes, and parsnips, so they finish cooking simultaneously.

Souper Saver

Keep prepped ingredients separate until you are ready to use them. It's handy to put them in individual bowls, disposable plastic bags from the market, or in piles on a baking sheet or cutting board. You might want to cover cut vegetables with a damp paper towel to prevent them from withering.

Measuring Up

You may not think measuring is that important. After all, on TV cooking shows the chef just flings a bit of this and some of that into the pot, and it works out great. Two things—nobody is going to eat that TV-set food, which is possibly misted with a lot of vegetable oil or sprayed with unnamable chemicals to give it the right look under the lights. And more than likely, the TV chef is experienced, and experience allows anyone, including you, to have free rein.

Imagine if you didn't measure correctly and put in 2 tablespoons of curry and $1/2$ teaspoon of cayenne when all you needed was 2 teaspoons of curry and a $1/4$ teaspoon of cayenne? Not the end of the world, but probably far too spicy (so to repair, you make another batch, very lightly spiced, and combine the two). Suppose you add $3^1/2$ cups of broth instead of $2^1/2$ cups—perhaps the soup will be too thin. Sometimes these mistakes work out, but if you're a beginning cook, that's not always the case. It's good to know how and what to measure so you have a better chance of getting consistently good results, even when you feel like experimenting in your kitchen lab.

Measuring cups come in both dry and liquid measure. You'll need both to do the job accurately. Don't forget, wet and dry measuring cups aren't interchangeable, and you'll need both. Fortunately, cooking (more than baking) is in general far more forgiving of sloppy measuring—something we're all prone to when we're in a hurry.

➤ Glass and clear plastic measuring cups are used for liquids. They generally come in 1-, 2-, and 4-cup measures. Set the measures on a countertop and pour in the ingredient. Check it by bending over to see at eye level whether the liquid rises to the correct line. Some folks hold the cup in the air and pour—this is one way to make sure your measurement will definitely be off the mark.

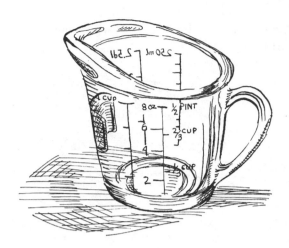

liquid measuring cup

➤ Dry measuring cups are made of metal or plastic and come in sets of $^1/_4$-, $^1/_3$-, $^1/_2$-, and 1-cup sizes, although occasionally you can get a $^1/_8$-cup (a coffee measure) or a 2-cup measure as well. Spoon the dry ingredients into the cup, rather than dipping the cup into an ingredient, and then level off the top with the flat side of a knife or spatula. That way you'll get an accurate measure. Although it's not as important with things like chopped vegetables, fruit, or nuts, it is crucial that flour and other dry ingredients be measured this way.

dry measuring cups

➤ Measuring spoon sets are also graded from $^1/_4$ teaspoon, $^1/_2$ teaspoon, 1 teaspoon, and 1 tablespoon. Some sets also include a $^1/_2$-tablespoon measure, which is equivalent to $1^1/_2$ teaspoons. It's easy to do $^1/_8$ teaspoon: just fill a $^1/_4$-teaspoon measure halfway. A pinch or a dash is less than $^1/_8$ teaspoon. When measuring ingredients with spoons, try to keep the ingredients level to the top, neither

69

lower than the top nor heaping over it. It will make quite a difference when you're measuring spices.

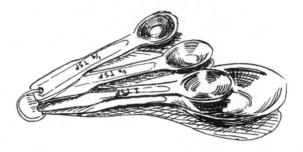

spoon set

Get Cooking!

Your *mise en place* is all set. Before you actually begin cooking, read the recipe again to reacquaint yourself with all the steps and their proper sequence. Take a moment to get it clear in your mind and make a few notes if you feel so inclined. Keep the recipe nearby, and let it be a handy reference to look at as you need to.

The Least You Need to Know

➤ Read the recipe thoroughly.

➤ Assemble all the equipment and ingredients before you begin cooking.

➤ Cut like ingredients into same-size pieces.

➤ Use the proper utensils to measure ingredients accurately.

Chapter 9

Soup Techniques

All soups aren't made alike. Sometimes ingredients are sautéed first, and other times everything's put into the pot at once. Some soups are made with broth, others with water. What's consistent is that soup and broth should be gently simmered, never boiled. Boiling puts any impurities, such as fat or scum that have risen to the surface, back into the soup. It also makes proteins like meat stringier or tougher, and boiling can evaporate too much of the liquid, letting solid ingredients scorch or stick to the bottom of the pot. Although soup or broth may be brought up to a boil, the heat should then be reduced so the liquid simmers or bubbles gently. The pot should be covered, partially covered, or left uncovered as the recipes indicate.

Broth Techniques: Homemade, Canned, and Cubes

There's nothing like homemade broth. It's wholesome and rich-tasting on it's own, and it's the substructure of many wonderful soups. Recipes for several standard broths in Part 5, Chapter 13 are those you will generally use whenever you want homemade taste.

Broth is made by simmering water with the flesh and bones of poultry, meat, and fish along with a few vegetables or simply by simmering a combination of vegetables. The liquid is then strained and becomes the base for various soups. In the traditional definition, stocks are generally prepared from just bones, not flesh, and vegetable trimmings. For the purposes of most cookbooks and recipes, the words broth and stock usually refer to the same thing—a flavored liquid made from poultry, fish, or meat, and/or vegetables.

Meat, poultry, and fish broth should have a minimum of seasoning, such as a bouquet garni, or contain aromatic vegetables, such as carrots, celery, onions, or leeks, but the broth never should be salted. Some cooks like to add salt while cooking vegetable broth, but I think it's wiser to wait and add salt at the end of a soup recipe.

Souper Clue

Make a batch of broth and freeze it. That way you'll have it on hand when you need it.

Homemade Broth Rules

➤ When making broth, always start with cold water.

➤ For the most flavor, the water should cover the solid ingredients by a few inches, but not be too deep or the broth will be thin and flavorless.

➤ Skim off fat and foam from the surface during the cooking process. Use a ladle or a skimmer.

➤ Simmer, don't boil.

➤ If the broth is too bland, simmer it a bit longer to reduce it and concentrate the flavor.

➤ If it's too strong, add extra water.

➤ Strain the broth through a fine-meshed sieve. Do not press on the ingredients in the sieve. The only exception is vegetable stock: to extract the greatest degree of vegetable flavor, press the vegetables in the sieve gently with the back of a spoon.

➤ Use broth immediately or chill it fast, then refrigerate it (see p. 81).

➤ Remove fat by chilling or by using a gravy separator.

Other than Homemade: Canned and Instant

In all honesty, I don't always have the time to make homemade broth. Sometimes I feel like making soup and don't have the time or the inclination to thaw what's in my freezer. For convenience, use prepared broth. Some supermarkets sell "freshly made" chicken broth that they keep refrigerated or frozen and that's almost as good as homemade.

Most of the time, I, like many other people with busy lives, use canned broth. Try to purchase low-sodium versions that are available in the soup aisle or in health food or diet sections of supermarkets. Although they are less salty then the regular version,

skimmer

they still tend to be far more salty than homemade broths, so the soup you make with them won't need much additional salt, if any.

Bouillon cubes are notoriously high in sodium and should only be used if nothing else is available. Although there are some higher quality cubes sold in health food stores, most bouillon cubes lack the depth of flavor found in homemade, or even in canned, broth.

I rarely salt any soup I've made with cubes. To cut the salt, I might alter the ratio of cubes to water, using a cup more water per cube than the amount indicated on the package. The vegetables or meat in the soup create additional flavor and make up for using fewer cubes. Whatever kind you end up using—homemade, canned or cubes—due to convenience or necessity, pay attention to the saltiness of the broth and use caution so your finished soup isn't too salty to eat.

Fancy Brown Broth

The term *brown broth* used to refer only to rich-tasting meat broth. The meaty bones and the vegetables used in the broth were roasted before being simmered, a process which makes the flavor deeper and fuller, and the color a dark, appetizing

Souper Idea

Eliminate excess fat in homemade broth and soup by cooling it to lukewarm and refrigerating it for several hours or overnight. The fat will solidify on the surface and can be removed easily.

Souper Clue

To deglaze a roasting pan, pour about 1 to 1 1/2 cups hot or boiling water into the pan. Scrape the bottom with a wooden spoon to loosen any browned bits. Use this liquid in broth and sauces, strained or not as indicated in the recipe.

73

brown. But brown broth doesn't have to include meat. You can make a roasted-vegetable broth and a brown chicken broth besides the more traditional beef broth. Don't use this method for fish or shellfish broth, which should be light in color.

Roasted or browned broths take longer to make but have a more robust taste. Once you've mastered the basic broth recipes (see Chapter 13), you might want to try making browned broth when you have extra time.

Browned Chicken Broth

Easy to Intermediate $3^1/_2$ to $4^1/_2$ hours
Freezes well for 4 to 6 months   Makes about $2^1/_2$ quarts

5 pounds chicken parts, (necks, backs, thighs, and wings)

2 medium carrots, unpeeled and cut into chunks

1 medium onion, peeled and halved

3 celery stalks with leaves attached, cut into chunks

$1^1/_2$ teaspoons black peppercorns

1 bay leaf

4 sprigs parsley

4 to 5 quarts water, or enough to cover

1. Roast the bones and parts at 400°F for 40 to 50 minutes or until lightly browned, turning them a few times during the roasting process and making sure the bones don't burn. Add the vegetables after 20 minutes.

2. After the bones and veggies are browned, transfer them to a large soup or stock pot. Deglaze the roasting pan with water. Add the rich brown liquid to the pot.

3. Cover the meat or vegetables with water. Over medium-high heat, bring the liquid to a boil. Skim off any foam. After the liquid boils, reduce the heat to medium-low.

4. Simmer for 3 to 4 hours, skimming the fat and foam every half hour or so. Add additional water if too much has evaporated.

5. Strain the broth and discard the solids. Use immediately or cool, uncovered, by placing the pot in an ice bath and stirring the broth, then refrigerate it for several hours or overnight and remove any solidified fat. Use within 2 to 3 days or freeze.

For **Browned Beef Broth:**   Follow the Browned Chicken Broth recipe, but use $2^1/_2$ pounds of chicken parts and $2^1/_2$ pounds of meaty beef bones or oxtails. Follow the instructions for Browned Chicken Broth but increase the roasting time to 45 minutes to 1 hour, adding the vegetables after 20 minutes.

Roasted or Browned Vegetable Broth

Easy   1½ to 2 hours   Freezes well for 4 to 6 months   Makes about 2 quarts

1 large potato, cut into chunks

2 medium carrots, cut into chunks

1 to 2 small parsnips, cut into chunks

2 celery stalks with leaves attached, cut into chunks

2 medium leeks, washed and cut into chunks

1 medium onion, sliced

1⅓ cups mushroom stems, not shiitake, optional

3 sprigs parsley

1 bay leaf

1 teaspoon black peppercorns

2½ to 3 quarts water

1. Roast the vegetables in a 400°F oven for 25 to 45 minutes, turning the vegetables occasionally so they don't burn.

2. After the veggies are browned, transfer them to a large soup or stock pot. Deglaze the roasting pan with water. Add the rich brown liquid to the pot.

3. Cover the vegetables with water. Over medium-high heat, bring the liquid to a boil. When the liquid boils, reduce the heat to medium-low and simmer about 50 to 60 minutes.

4. Strain the broth and press gently on the vegetables in the sieve with the back of a wooden spoon. Discard the solid ingredients. Use the broth immediately or cool, uncovered, by placing the pot in an ice bath and stirring the broth; then refrigerate it. Use within 3 days or freeze.

Basic Techniques: To Sauté or Not to Sauté

Many well-prepared soups start with a quick sauté of aromatic vegetables—onions, leeks, carrots, celery, or scallions. Sautéing helps to release the full taste as well as the natural sugars in the vegetables, making them sweeter. Fragrant flavor enhancers such as garlic, ginger, chilies, lemon grass, or spices that require cooking to unlock their taste are most often added after the aromatic vegetables begin to soften. These sautéed ingredients create a delicious layer of flavor for the soup. This preparation method is often used in pureed soups as well as in some vegetable and poultry soups.

After sautéing, add to the pot wet ingredients such as tomatoes, wine, broth or other liquid. Other ingredients such as vegetables are added, and the liquid is brought to a boil. The heat is then reduced so the soup simmers gently until it is finished.

You'll also find recipes in which ingredients are combined in the pot with liquid without sautéing at all. Again, the liquid is brought to a boil and the heat is reduced so the soup simmers. It's a different kind of culinary brew, but equally tasty. You might find this process used more often in some hearty ethnic soups, such as those based on legumes.

Souper Bowl Fact

Sauté is a French word that means to jump but it also refers to a fundamental cooking process. To sauté, in a pot over medium heat, melt butter or margarine or heat a small amount of vegetable or olive oil. Add the ingredients and cook, stirring vegetables occasionally or turning meat only once or twice. Don't overcrowd the pan or the food will steam.

Souper Bowl Fact

Did you know there is a term for the combination of chopped aromatic vegetables, such as onions, celery, and carrots, found in many soups and sauces? The French call it **mirepoix,** the Spanish call it **sofrito** (and they add pork fat and annatto seeds for a red color), and Italians call it **soffrito** (they tend to add green peppers). Sometimes garlic is added after a few minutes. Sometimes the carrots are omitted and leeks are added. Creole and Cajun cooking uses a combination of onion, scallions, and green bell peppers.

Seasoning Soup with Whole Herbs and Spices

Many recipes call for whole spices or herbs that can be picked out by the cook or the diner. Some cultures consider it good luck when a portion contains a whole spice. If you prefer not to serve whole spices or herbs in your soup, you can remove them with a slotted spoon or use a small, tea-size, fine-mesh strainer to remove them.

You can also make a bouquet garni by wrapping the whole herbs or spices in a small piece of cheesecloth, or in the rinsed leaf of a leek, and tie it securely before adding it. Remove the bouquet garni before serving. In a pinch you can put the herbs in a small metal tea ball and add it into the broth. Sometimes whole herbs or spices are sautéed with vegetables, before the addition of broth, to bring out their fullest flavor. After sautéing, remove them with a slotted spoon, wrap them in cheesecloth, and return the sack to the pot with the broth.

making a bouquet garni

Salting the Soup

When making broth, soup, and stews or any long-simmering item, don't salt the food until near or at the end of the cooking time. The reason for this is that some of the liquid always evaporates and it's hard to gauge precisely the final intensity of the salt in the soup. If you use a canned broth, it already contains salt, which will become stronger as the soup simmers. If you salt at the beginning, the salt taste will become more potent and you'll end up with soup that's overseasoned.

You'll notice that the recipes don't specify the amount of salt, but make a suggestion. This isn't an oversight or a trick. I don't know whether you're using homemade, regular canned, low-sodium canned, or cubed broth, which all have different sodium contents. Taste the soup at the end; add the salt in small amounts. You can always add more but you can't take it out once it's in.

Fixing Soup Faux Pas

Well, you were supposed to simmer slowly and you had the heat so high the liquid evaporated while you were relaxing in the tub or in front of the tube. So you've added too much salt—oops. Another time, you forgot to put the cover on the pot, or covered it and it's boiled over, spilling some of the precious broth onto the stove top. Maybe you've simmered it on too low a heat and it needs a little

Souper Clue

Most soup will require between $1/2$ and 1 teaspoon of salt, but taste!

extra cooking for the ingredients to be tender, or the soup is not as thick as you like it. What do you do now? Here are a few remedies for these common mistakes.

It's Too Salty

➤ If it's only a little bit salty, add additional broth or water and simmer a while longer.

➤ Add a peeled, raw potato that has been quartered, and simmer for 15 minutes. Remove the potato with a slotted spoon and discard before serving. The potato will absorb some of the salt.

➤ Trick your tastebuds by adding sugar, starting with 1/4 teaspoon, until the soup tastes less salty.

➤ If you have time, make a second batch without salt and combine the two. Taste and adjust salt (be careful this time!). You'll definitely have soup for your freezer.

It's Too Thick

➤ Add additional broth, water, milk, or whatever liquid is used for the soup. Simmer until it's heated through and the flavor is balanced.

It's Too Thin

➤ Increase the heat slightly and simmer, uncovered, until it's the right consistency. Don't boil the soup rapidly.

➤ Puree some of the ingredients in the soup in a blender or food processor and return them to the pot.

➤ Add mild-tasting, pureed vegetables, such as mashed potatoes, or ingredients such as pureed cooked rice (puree the rice in the blender with some of the soup) or fresh bread crumbs.

➤ If it's a pureed soup, add additional pureed vegetables already called for in the recipe.

➤ If only slightly thin, change the texture and make it creamy by adding cream or a dollop of sour cream or yogurt.

Boiled Over or Undercooked

➤ If the soup's boiled over, first turn off the burner and clean up the mess so it doesn't bake into the surface of the stove. Then return the soup to the heat and add enough broth to make the desired consistency. Reduce the heat to medium-low and simmer, partially covered, until the flavors are blended. Taste for seasoning and adjust.

➤ If the soup's undercooked, more than likely the heat's been too low for too long a period. This sometimes happens with electric stoves when currents fluctuate. Increase the heat slightly and continue simmering until the ingredients are tender and the soup acquires the right consistency.

The Least You Need to Know

➤ Simmer soup and broth, don't boil.

➤ Sautéing vegetables increases their sweetness and flavor.

➤ Salt soup at the end of cooking.

➤ If the soup's too salty, add a quartered, peeled potato and simmer for 15 minutes, then remove and discard the potato.

➤ If the soup's too thin, thicken it by simmering longer, or by adding mashed potatoes or unseasoned bread crumbs.

Chapter 10

Soup Safety

In This Chapter

➤ How to chill broth and soup safely

➤ How to store and freeze broth and soup

➤ How to thaw and reheat safely

Food follows the golden rule: the way you treat it is the way it'll end up treating you. After you finish cooking a broth or soup, you might not want to use it or eat it right away. Perhaps you want to keep it for later in the week or freeze it. But don't just let it sit on the back of the stove. It's very important to handle any food properly to prevent bacterial growth, and broth is no exception. Don't fret—there are a few easy steps you can take to prevent any potential contamination.

➤ Broth, as well as meat, poultry, vegetable, and creamy soups can be refrigerated for up to three days.

➤ Vegetable purees and legume soups can be refrigerated for up to four days.

Chilling Safely

It's unwise to put any food, especially hot broth or soup, directly into the refrigerator or freezer. The residual heat will raise the temperature of the fridge, and not only the soup but also other items can spoil. It's important to chill it quickly, though. If you keep broth or soup at room temperature for too long, it becomes a breeding ground for bacteria. Here are some easy steps for keeping food safe and tasting its best:

➤ To cool broth, fill a kitchen sink one-third full with very cold water. Add a couple of trays of ice cubes to the water to make it frigid. Put the pot directly into this ice-water bath, but be careful that the water doesn't spill over into the pot. This step is essential for broth that you're not using right away. Soup doesn't always require an ice-water bath unless you've made a big batch because you'll probably eat a portion right away. If, however, you're only storing the soup for a future meal, ice it down! An ice-water bath makes broth and soup, as well as stew, cool down faster for storage.

Souper Clue

Excess fat will solidify on the surface when the broth or soup is cold. The fat actually seals and protects it from bacteria. Leave the fat until you're ready to use the broth, then remove and discard it before heating. If you're planning to freeze the soup or broth, leave the fat on top as an extra guard against freezer burn, and remove it after thawing.

➤ Use a ladle or spoon to stir the broth or soup until it cools down to lukewarm—cool enough that you can poke your clean finger in it and it doesn't feel hot. When you stir the soup, bring the liquid from the bottom to the top, so the temperature reduces evenly and more quickly.

➤ Transfer the cooled broth or soup to another container that it fills completely, and cover it.

➤ If you've made soup in a stainless or enamel-coated pot, once it's cooled you can put the covered pot in the fridge for a few hours or overnight, and transfer the soup to a more suitable container the next morning.

➤ Promptly refrigerate or freeze cooled broth or soup.

Storage Containers

What's the best vessel to store broth or soup in? Here's a breakdown:

➤ **For refrigerator storage:** use a stainless steel, plastic, porcelain, or glass container, covered with a tight-fitting lid or plastic wrap.

➤ **For freezer storage:** use self-sealing freezer bags or freezer-proof plastic containers with lids that have a tight seal.

➤ Don't store broth or soup in aluminum or cast iron because they will impart an unpleasant or metallic taste to the food.

Freezing Basics

Freezing is the most convenient way to store leftovers for future meals. A few practical tips can help you freeze correctly:

➤ When the broth or soup is cooled, you can transfer it to freezer-proof containers.

➤ Use containers that are the right size—individual portions for quick meals, and pint or quart size for larger batches.

➤ Food expands when it freezes. Ideally, broth or soup should nearly fill its container. Ladle soup into the container so there is a $1/2$- to 1-inch gap at the top.

➤ Close the container, open it partially to release any trapped or excess air, and then seal well. If using self-sealing bags, release any air, then seal and fold the top of the bag flat against the liquid to release any remaining excess air.

Souper Clue

Some people like to freeze broth in ice cube trays and keep the resulting broth cubes in a self-sealing plastic bag. You can combine a few cubes for a warming cup of broth. They're also great for recipes where you need only a small amount, such as sauces.

Here's a timetable of how long broth and soup can be frozen:

Type of Soup	Time
Broth	Up to 6 months
Pureed vegetable soups	Up to 3 months
Legume soups	Up to 2 months
Creamy soups	Up to 2 months
Brothy, multi-ingredient soups	1 to 2 months
Seafood soups	Best eaten fresh or within 3 days

Thawing

There are a few ways to thaw soup. All work equally well; some are just faster.

➤ Thaw overnight in the refrigerator.

➤ Thaw in the microwave, following the directions for your unit.

➤ Thaw, uncovered, on the counter until softened and liquid, then reheat or finish thawing in the refrigerator.

Souper Saver

If the lid has popped off in the freezer, you probably overfilled the container. In most cases, freezer burn has developed. The surface will look cracked and possibly parched. Often many ice crystals will have formed on top. Food with freezer burn will taste "off" and should be discarded.

Simple Suggestions for Reheating

➤ Reheat broth and soup over medium heat, stirring occasionally.

➤ Bring broth and soup to a boil to kill off any bacteria that may have accumulated if it was stored improperly, then reduce the heat and simmer.

➤ If any ingredients start sticking, stir and reduce the heat to medium-low.

The Least You Need to Know

➤ Chill broth quickly in an ice-water bath in the sink to prevent any possible bacterial growth. Stir both broth and soup with a spoon or ladle until cooled, then refrigerate.

➤ Store broth or soup in plastic, ceramic, glass, or stainless steel containers with tight-fitting lids. Don't use cast iron or aluminum.

➤ Leave $1/2$- to 1-inch expansion room in any freezer container.

➤ Thaw frozen food in the microwave, or overnight in the fridge.

Chapter 11

Playing with Your Food

In This Chapter

➤ Learn a few techniques for improvising

➤ How and when you can substitute—and with what ingredients

➤ Use less fat, but have full flavor

Be honest. Who doesn't like to play with their food? Whether out of a sense of adventure—how would curry taste?—or from sheer necessity—the store was out of green beans—making up a dish is the uncharted territory all of us enter at one time or another. When it comes to soup, this is certainly not a new or radical process, but actually a well-established tradition throughout Europe, particularly in parts of France and Switzerland. There, in home and restaurant kitchens alike, the soup pot is always simmering on the stove, and cooks add ingredients daily, some fresh, some leftovers, altering the combinations to create a new soup du jour—every day!

Improvising and substituting ingredients can be both a daunting and rewarding event, but by all means let it be fun. Your experience is certainly a help, and common sense is your biggest ally when embarking on this culinary journey into the unknown. Perhaps you won't want to try it when company's coming, but maybe that depends on who's coming. I can offer a few hints that will get you started and point you in the right direction, and after that you're on your own. With a little practice, you too will be able to make your own concoctions.

Perhaps you want to try to imitate something you've eaten in a restaurant, or perhaps you just want to let your own imagination go wild. Browse through a few recipes, check your kitchen inventory, and get going.

My only advice: "Keep it simple." The flavors should be pure, clean, and fresh. This is not the time to try to become an expert on ethnic or cross-cultural cuisine by combining spices and herbs you're unsure of, or to blend Asian ingredients with Italian. When the soup is finished and you like it, and your friends rave about your culinary talents, your worry lines will vanish. You may even consider doing it again.

Halving and Doubling Recipes

Changing the quantity you make may be one of your first improvisations. Let's say you would like to make some lentil or bean soup, but you don't want to make a full batch because you only want it today and your freezer compartment is already overloaded. Or perhaps you're having a crowd and want to make a double batch. Here's the hitch—recipes don't always scale up or scale down in perfect proportion. You'll need to make a few minor adjustments.

Halving

When halving a recipe, be aware that you might need to alter the seasonings as well as the amount of liquid. Start with half the specified quantity and add a little more if necessary. The cooking time might also be a little less than if you were making a full recipe, so pay closer attention while it simmers. If the recipe starts with sautéed onions, you might need a bit more than half the vegetable oil or butter.

Souper Clue

When halving or doubling a recipe, sometimes having unused raw veggies is unavoidable. If the ingredient list states 1 medium onion, chopped, or 1 medium carrot, chopped—why keep half an onion or carrot in the fridge when you can use a small one instead? Conversely, if double the amount requires 4 celery stalks and 2 cups of green beans, but you only have 3 celery stalks and 2$^1/_4$ cups of green beans, use what you have and keep going.

Doubling

When doubling a recipe, make sure you have a pot that's large enough, or divide the mixture evenly in two pots. You'll probably need to adjust the cooking time. If you use a very large pot, the cooking time will definitely increase, because it will take longer for the liquid to come to a boil.

If you're making the soup in one large pot you won't need to double the amount of vegetable oil or butter, but use only slightly more. You'll also need to check the amount of liquid while it's cooking to see whether you need to add some more or perhaps take out a ladleful, keeping what you removed handy in the event you actually do need to return it to the pot.

Don't just double the seasonings. Taste the soup as it cooks. Ingredients such as bay leaves don't necessarily need to be doubled at all—you can get by with 1 or 1$^1/_2$ at most. If the soup has fresh chilies, you might want to try it with 1$^1/_2$ times the amount. The same goes for cayenne pepper or chili powder.

Salt and pepper are the biggest challenges—there is no direct scale up here. Remember to add them in small increments and taste, taste, taste. Changing the quantity is not really that difficult, but it does require a little extra attention. You'll soon get the hang of it.

How to Make Pureed Soups

Pureed vegetable soups are a snap to make and allow you to take advantage of whatever is in your fridge. Think about what might taste good together or what ingredients you've combined in recipes that you've already mastered. Look and see what you have on hand and set your mind free to come up with some suggestions. You might make a flop, but you might make a winner!

Souper Clue

When halving or doubling a recipe, write the ingredient list on a piece of paper with the quantities you will be using. It's too easy to make a mistake if you simply do it in your head as you go along.

Making the Most of What You Have

If you have some fresh vegetables you'd like to turn into a pureed soup, sauté an onion, carrot, and celery stalk, add a bit of white wine (or not), and some broth. Bring the liquid to a boil, and add the vegetables and herbs or spices. Reduce the heat and simmer until the veggies are tender. Puree with a hand blender or in batches in a food processor or blender. Thicken any soups, if necessary, by adding mashed potatoes or by adding up to $1/2$ cup cooked rice to the soup before pureeing. Add cream, sour cream, or yogurt and season with salt and pepper.

Leftover Remakes

Have a little fun. You have bowls of leftover veggies that are great material for your concoction—some cooked potatoes, cauliflower, carrots, and green beans. Maybe you have some rice leftover from a Chinese takeout and half a head of lettuce, or yesterday's zucchini and scallion stir-fry with a hint of ginger. Here are the basic ingredients for two potential soups, both different. Why not simmer each set of ingredients in some chicken or vegetable broth, add a few herbs such as thyme or parsley or chives to the first set, and puree each with a hand blender or in the food processor. Add a little milk or cream to the first soup, maybe a hint of sherry or soy sauce to the second. Taste for seasoning. Two homemade soups, and almost as fast as opening a can.

Souper Saver

Leftovers are already seasoned with salt, pepper, and other herbs or spices. Keep this in mind when you combine them in soup so you don't mix conflicting flavors. Taste and use a light hand when seasoning the soup.

Everything's In It but the Kitchen Sink...

Sometimes you don't feel like following a recipe. You want to make soup, and you can make a simple soup. Your best bet is to skim through several recipes before you begin. Get some ideas and inspiration.

Souper Clue

If you want to use items that cook quickly, such as shrimp, fish, snow peas, and the like, make sure you add them toward the end of the cooking time. Whether raw or cooked, these items take only a few minutes.

Here's a suggestion: start with the aromatic vegetable combination—chopped onion, carrot, celery, or one of its variations with bell pepper or scallions or leeks—and sauté them in a tablespoon or two of olive or vegetable oil. Add a clove or two of minced garlic. Add the broth, vegetables and/or meat, or leftover cooked poultry and some noodles or rice. Bring the liquid to a boil, reduce the heat so the soup simmers, and cover partially. Simmer until everything is cooked through.

You've Got Great Timing

Timing isn't everything, but it sure helps when it comes to improvisation, so you don't end up with uncooked food or mush. When putting ingredients together think of how long each item takes to cook individually, then add them to your soup in the correct order.

Ballpark Timing for a Few Common Ingredients

Ingredient	Cooking Time
Rice, white	15 to 20 minutes
Brown and wild rice	45 to 55 minutes
Pearl barley	45 to 55 minutes
Pasta and noodles, dried fresh	8 to 12 minutes 2 to 8 minutes
Potatoes and sweet potatoes, cubed	15 to 30 minutes, depending on size
Dried lentils	15 to 45 minutes, depending on type
Dried beans and split peas	$1^1/_2$ to 2 hours (plus any soaking time)
Root vegetables, cubed	15 to 35 minutes, depending on size
Beets	35 minutes to 1 hour, depending on size
Cabbage	40 minutes to 1 hour
Broccoli and cauliflower	10 minutes for just-tender and crunchy, up to 45 minutes if for puree
Butternut squash, peeled and cubed	20 to 25 minutes
Spinach, snow peas, sugar snap peas	2 to 5 minutes

Ingredient	Cooking Time
Zucchini, yellow squash, green beans	5 to 12 minutes, depending on size
Carrots and celery	Up to 25 to 30 minutes
Tomatoes, fresh	Up to 30 to 35 minutes
Chicken parts, raw boneless	30 to 50 minutes 15 to 25 minutes
Cooked chicken	10 to 15 minutes
Beef or lamb cubes, raw	$1^1/_2$ to 2 hours
Shrimp, raw	5 minutes
Fish, raw	10 to 15 minutes

Substitute Teacher

What do you do when you dislike a particular ingredient in a recipe or you're out of an item? Substitute, of course, replacing it with something that you enjoy eating. Try to use an ingredient that has a similar texture and cooking time.

Ingredient	Substitution
Boneless, skinless chicken breasts	Boneless, skinless chicken thighs
Cooked, shredded, or cubed chicken	Cooked, shredded, or cubed turkey
Beef bottom round, cubed	Beef chuck, cubed
Firm white fish	Cod, scrod, halibut, haddock, catfish
Soft white fish	Flounder, sea bass, sole, trout
Butternut squash	Acorn squash
Cauliflower or broccoli	Brocco-flower
Savoy cabbage	Green cabbage
Snow peas	Sugar snap peas
Green beans	Wax beans
Zucchini	Yellow squash
Sweet potatoes	Yams, butternut squash, or potatoes
Potatoes	Baby potatoes or sweet potatoes
Turnips	Rutabaga or parsnips
Spinach	Swiss chard, sorrel, or watercress
Bell peppers	Use colors interchangeably
Romaine lettuce	Escarole
Small pasta shells	Small macaroni or ditalini

continues

Ingredient	Substitution
Thin egg noodles	Angel hair, fideos, or ramen
White rice	Basmati rice
Tomatoes, skinned, seeded, chopped	Canned tomatoes, chopped or whole, broken up with a spoon
Pureed tomatoes	Tomato sauce
Fresh corn, green beans, peas, or lima beans	Frozen vegetables
Dry beans, cooked	Canned beans, drained and rinsed
Dry white wine	Dry white vermouth
Salt	Salt substitute
Eggs	Egg substitute
Cream	Half-and-half, milk, 2% milk
Sour cream	Nonfat sour cream or yogurt
Apple juice	Apple cider or white grape juice

Souper Saver

If a recipe calls for wine or sherry, *never* substitute cooking wine or cooking sherry. They don't add a true wine taste and contain a large amount of sodium. A good rule for cooking with alcohol is not to cook with any wine you wouldn't also drink.

Make It Vegetarian

Sometimes you want to make a soup vegetarian—maybe a friend is coming over who doesn't eat meat. I often turn legume soups into vegetarian meals. Omit the ham hock or sausage and follow the instructions. You might want to add an extra clove of garlic or half a seeded, minced jalapeño, or a pinch more herbs in the beginning, or add a little extra salt or pepper to the soup after it's cooked.

It's simply not possible to convert hearty meat soups or fish soups. I've had wonderful success with many soups that don't contain meat, however, such as cream soups, vegetable purees, or vegetable soups that utilize chicken broth. These can easily become vegetarian delights. Replace the chicken broth with vegetable broth, mushroom broth, or roasted-vegetable broth. In some of the Asian soup recipes, I've already made suggestions to omit cooked shredded chicken and replace it with tofu.

Lighten Up with Less Fat

The recipes in the book use only the fat that's necessary for cooking and that will still let the finished soup taste its best. Due to dietary concerns, some people may still want or need to lighten up further. Here are a few general tips:

➤ Cook in nonstick pans. You can use slightly less vegetable or olive oil or butter than is called for.

➤ Trim meat and poultry of all visible fat.

➤ Replace full cream or half-and-half and whole milk products with low-fat, skim, or nonfat dairy products. Note that low-fat cheeses don't melt as smoothly, so they might not be a wise choice.

➤ Chill soup and broth and remove any visible fat from the surface. Reheat before serving. Chill canned broth as well, and remove any fat, minimal though it may be, before using.

Global Village Mix 'n' Match: Using Regional Ingredients

Many ingredients—such as meat, poultry, fish, onions, carrots and celery—are universal, and others are specific to certain countries or regions. Most cuisines combine certain items regularly and draw on flavorings from specific places to help bring the whole world to your table.

This useful guide offers suggestions for mixing foods and seasonings according to their ethnic heritage, whether you're being creative with just one recipe or planning an entire menu.

Northern Europe

➤ **Scandinavia:** sour cream, cream, butter, dill, nutmeg, cardamom, ginger, cheese, anchovies, pickled foods, beets

➤ **Russia, Poland, and Ukraine:** sour cream, beets, cabbage, potatoes, caraway, vinegar, mustard, kielbasa or sausage

➤ **Hungary:** sour cream, butter, paprika, marjoram, vinegar

➤ **Germany:** butter, potatoes, cabbage, cheese, beer, caraway, nutmeg, beets, vinegar

➤ **Holland and Belgium:** butter, cream, Gouda and Edam cheese, chervil, parsley, beer

➤ **United Kingdom:** butter, cream, Stilton blue and cheddar cheese, dried fish, potatoes

➤ **Northern France:** butter, cream, cheeses, flat-leaf parsley, wine, beer

The Mediterranean

➤ **Southern France—Provence:** wine, olive oil, garlic, thyme, tarragon, flat-leaf parsley, rosemary, basil, orange, almonds, Parmesan, pasta, black olives, roasted red peppers, tomatoes, orange, lemon, white beans

➤ **Greece:** olive oil, garlic, oregano, lemon, black olives, tomatoes, lemon

➤ **Italy:** wine, olive oil, garlic, flat-leaf parsley, basil, rosemary, pasta, polenta, hazelnuts, Parmesan, Romano, balsamic vinegar, anchovies, black olives, roasted red peppers, tomatoes, almonds, orange, lemon, white beans

➤ **Spain:** sherry, olive oil, green and black olives, garlic, bell peppers, tomatoes, chili peppers, paprika

➤ **Portugal:** port wine, chorizo, olive oil, chili peppers, paprika

➤ **Morocco:** cinnamon, cumin, honey, lemon, orange, chickpeas, tomatoes, saffron, cloves

The Americas

➤ **United States and Canada:** cranberries, wild rice, corn, maple syrup, turkey, clams, lobster, salmon, butternut squash or pumpkin

➤ **Southern US:** collards, sweet potatoes, peanuts, pecans, lima beans, corn, vinegar, whiskey, hominy, cornmeal

➤ **Cajun and Creole:** scallions, onions, bell pepper, celery, tomatoes, andouille sausage, Tabasco sauce, white pepper, cayenne, thyme, bay leaf, red beans, parsley, shrimp

➤ **Southwestern US:** chili powder, chili peppers, tomatoes, corn, cornmeal, beans, cilantro, oregano, garlic, cumin

➤ **Mexico:** chili peppers, almonds, chocolate, tomatoes, vanilla, sesame seeds, corn, cornmeal, beans, lime, avocado, butternut, cilantro, garlic, chorizo, oregano, cumin, turkey

➤ **Caribbean:** Scotch Bonnet peppers, coconut, mango, papaya, rum, allspice, cloves, cinnamon, thyme, ginger, garlic, sweet potatoes, pumpkin, rice

➤ **South America:** chili peppers, yams, peanuts, cumin, paprika, bell peppers, corn, potatoes, black beans

Africa

➤ **West Africa:** pumpkin, sweet potatoes, peanuts, chili peppers, collards, garlic, beans

➤ **South Africa:** wine, chili peppers, vinegar, cinnamon, allspice, cloves, coriander, curry powder, cumin, bay leaf, ginger, garlic, coconut milk, mint, cilantro, butternut, tomatoes, corn, hominy, rice, orange, tangerine

Asia

➤ **India:** chili peppers, ginger, garlic, cinnamon, cloves, turmeric, coriander, curry powder, garam masala, cumin, bay leaf, tomatoes, coconut, mint, cilantro, rice

➤ **Thailand:** lemon grass, garlic, ginger, chili peppers, fish sauce, holy basil, mint, cilantro, rice, scallions

➤ **Malaysia and Indonesia:** chili peppers, coconut, mango, papaya, brown sugar, vinegar, cilantro, soy sauce, cinnamon, cardamom, cloves, coriander, bay leaf, ginger, garlic, mint, cilantro, rice

➤ **China:** soy sauce, ginger, garlic, scallions, rice, egg and rice noodles, wood or cloud ear mushrooms, hoisin sauce, oyster sauce, sesame oil, chili oil

➤ **Japan:** soy sauce, daikon, miso, rice wine, rice wine vinegar, rice, rice noodles, udon noodles, mung bean noodles, ginger, garlic, scallions

---

The Least You Need to Know

➤ You may need to adjust the amount of liquid and seasonings when halving or doubling a recipe.

➤ You can substitute ingredients of similar texture.

➤ When improvising, keep it uncomplicated and simple. Combine flavors from the same ethnic background.

➤ Make it vegetarian by substituting vegetable or mushroom broth.

Part 4
From the Ladle to the Table

Getting food on the table takes some advance preparation. Serving is easiest if you decide beforehand where you're going to eat—kitchen, den, dining room, or patio—and how—on a TV tray, at the dining table, or at the breakfast bar. Set the table and assemble whatever bowls, underplates, utensils such as spoons and ladles, and any other serving pieces you might need. Are the soup bowls warmed? Are you having bread? Do you want to warm it and put it in a basket? Are you making a salad? Are the salad plates chilled; is the dressing made? Have all these items in place so when it's time to sit down, you don't have to rush to finish last-minute details, but can relax and enjoy the meal.

Chapter 12

It's Your Serve

In This Chapter

➤ The best ways to serve soup

➤ Making your food pretty

➤ Turning soup into a meal

Whether you're planning a casual supper or a formal dinner, presentation sets the tone. Consider which accompaniments will round out the menu and which garnishes you will use. These extra touches do make a difference.

Serving Soup

Hot Soups

There's nothing more comforting than a hot bowl of soup. The trick is to keep it that way. When serving hot soup, warm the bowls. One way is to heat them in a preheated, low oven (200° to 250°F) for a few minutes. If your oven is being used for something else, pour boiling water from a kettle into the bowls. Let them stand for several minutes. Throw out the water, dry the bowls, and ladle in the piping-hot soup immediately.

Chilled Soups

In summer, cold soups are refreshingly delightful. Chill the bowls in the refrigerator for an hour or more. Don't put them in the freezer unless they're freezer-proof—they might crack.

Which Bowl Do You Use?

Most people have sets of everyday china bowls and that's what they use for any food requiring a bowl, but there actually are bowls designated for specific soups. Some soups, such as broths and creamy purees, cool down more quickly than chunky soups, and the shape of the bowls helps keep the particular soup hot or chilled.

➤ Crocks are oven-proof bowls, sometimes with one or two handles, used specifically for French onion soup. They're also good for thick chowders and hearty legume soups.

➤ Double-handled, deep bowls with sloped sides are known as cream soup bowls and are used also for broth and consommé. You'll find these in some formal place settings.

➤ Soup plates are shallow bowls, often with a wide rim. They are perfect for chowders, vegetable soups, hearty or brothy soups with many ingredients. Some china sets include them so you'll find that they're often used for a wide variety of soups. Note that soup cools more quickly in this shape.

➤ Medium-size, deep bowls with sloped sides are excellent for keeping soup hot. Because they're also included in sets, they too are used for serving all kinds of soup. They're ideal for Asian noodle soups.

➤ Chinese soup bowls are usually porcelain and look like large rice bowls. They're deep, with sharply sloped sides and a flat bottom, and they usually rest on a small pedestal. These are perfect for hot and sour soup and other Asian soups.

➤ Japanese soup bowls have a shape similar to Chinese soup bowls, but they're slightly fuller with a more rounded bottom. Sometimes made of lacquerware, they most often have lids. They're fine for broth and miso soups.

➤ Tureens are large porcelain or ceramic serving bowls with lids, used specifically for serving soup at a buffet, on the sideboard, or at the table. Sometimes the lid has a cutout where a ladle can be inserted.

Souper Bowl Fact

Soup bowls should be placed on an underplate. The only exceptions are Chinese and Japanese soup bowls. Underplates are not only a convenient place to rest your spoon when you're finished, they also keep the table clean if some of the soup spills. If you're worried about the bowl sliding on the plate, put a lightly dampened cocktail napkin under the bowl.

Your Final Touch

Garnishes are the finishing flair you add before sending your masterpiece to the table. The simpler the garnish, the better, and a little bit is all that's required. You don't need to spend too much time preparing them. Think of them as punctuation, your exclamation point. They can be an accent of color, a contrasting texture, a spotlight on a flavor already in the dish, or a distinct but complementary taste.

Garnishing Guide

General garnishes include chopped parsley and chives, but here are a few suggestions for garnishes that can be made in minutes:

➤ Finely chopped herbs or small sprigs such as basil, celery leaves, chervil, chives, cilantro, snipped dill, mint, or parsley

➤ Freshly ground spices such as coriander, nutmeg, black pepper, or white pepper

➤ Finely ground spices such as cayenne, cinnamon, garam masala, or paprika

➤ Fresh spices, aromatics, and chilies cut into thin strips or minced and used sparingly, such as ginger or seeded jalapeños, serranos, or cayenne chili peppers

➤ Tabasco or other liquid hot chili sauce

➤ Crushed red chili flakes

➤ Vegetables, finely diced or cut into thin strips, such as bell peppers, cucumber, scallions, or seeded tomatoes

➤ Homemade bacon bits

➤ Pesto

➤ Finely chopped sundried tomatoes mixed with a clove of minced garlic and a tablespoon of parsley and basil and a little cream or olive oil to bind

➤ Freshly grated cheese such as Parmesan or Romano, or crumbled blue, goat, or feta cheese

➤ Chopped hard-boiled eggs

➤ Yogurt or sour cream

➤ Cream or whipped cream

➤ Nuts such as chopped peanuts or slivered almonds

➤ Croutons

➤ Croutes (a thick slice of toasted or fried bread)

➤ Citrus wedges

➤ Finely grated citrus zest, or orange, lemon, or lime zest cut into very thin strips

Souper Clue

Appropriate garnishes are suggested in the recipes, but feel free to improvise. Choose a garnish that reflects, accentuates, balances, or complements the flavors and colors in the dish. Remember ethnic origins and don't put a dollop of sour cream into miso soup or sprinkle cilantro and chili flakes on borscht.

Souper Meals

Today's dining style is relaxed. Whether you're planning a meal for yourself, your family, or your company, creating a menu is easy. Put one together that will give you pleasure. Why not shoot for the stars? Ideally you should have as much enjoyment making it as you have eating it.

➤ **Soup as a first course:** In general, if your main course is light, such as grilled chicken or fish, start with a more substantial soup. If the main course is heavier, such as steak or chops, begin with a light soup. Serve it with rolls or crackers. As a first course, plan on $1/2$ cup to 1 cup per person. Hearty soups should not be served as a first course, but only as a main course because they are quite substantial.

➤ **Soup as a main course:** When serving soup as a main course, allow extra portions for second helpings. Naturally, your serving size will go up to 1 to 2 cups. Crisp and colorful greens, grilled or chopped vegetables, fresh fruit salad, as well as good crusty bread, rolls, and foccacia are perfect partners to most soup. You can stretch a light or a hearty soup to feed more people by offering sandwiches, a pasta salad, quiche, or an antipasto platter of cheese, fruit, marinated or grilled vegetables, cold meats, or smoked fish as well as an assortment of bread and crackers.

Souper Clue

When planning a meal, keep it practical and simple. Combine items of similar ethnic origins whose flavors work in harmony.

The Least You Need to Know

➤ Heat or chill your soup bowls.

➤ Keep garnishes simple, with colors and flavors that accent the dish, and use a light hand.

➤ Serve light soups for first courses, heartier soups for entrees.

Part 5
The Recipes

It's time to get your soup pot simmering. The following section offers a wide range of recipes, and there's sure to be one that will fit your mood, taste, budget, and schedule. Most of the ingredients are easily found in any good supermarket. A few recipes call for more unusual ingredients, but they're all available in ethnic groceries or specialty shops.

The recipes are coded by skill level. "Easy" recipes are just that—a snap—and any beginner can make them. "Intermediate" recipes require a bit more attention, although they're not difficult. "Challenging" indicates that there's a step or process that you must follow carefully or you might be in the soup instead of eating it, so you'd better turn off the TV.

Any special equipment you'll need, such as a food processor, blender, or hand blender, is clearly marked in the recipe headnotes. There's also an indication of the time it should take to make the soup. Cooking and chilling times present an accurate range. I also mention a prep time, which is the time it took me to prepare the raw ingredients prior to cooking—it might take you a few minutes longer when you're trying a recipe for the first time.

Here's a final reminder—read the recipe through before you begin cooking. Soon you'll be able to say, "Soup's on!"

FOUNTAIN OF SOUP

Chapter 13

Liquid Foundations

In This Chapter

➤ Chicken Broth

➤ Beef Broth

➤ Vegetable Broth

➤ Mushroom Broth

➤ Fish Broth

➤ Shrimp Broth

➤ Clam Broth

➤ Basic Dashi

Tasty on its own, a good broth is the basis for a great soup as well as for stews and sauces. It's not difficult to make, but requires time. Unlike commercially processed canned broths or bouillon cubes, all these broth recipes are salt-free. When making soup with homemade broth, adjust the salt to your taste. After the broth is made, strain with a fine-meshed sieve or a medium sieve lined with cheesecloth. Broth kept longer than two to three days must be frozen or brought back to a vigorous boil and chilled again. It will then last for another two to three days in the refrigerator. When storing broth, chill according to the directions on p. 81.

Chicken Broth

I like to make a lot of chicken broth at once and keep it on hand in my freezer. If you prefer, make a smaller amount by cutting this recipe in half. See p. 74 for a richer-flavored Browned Chicken Broth.

If your pot is too small to hold the full recipe, make less or divide the batch and cook in more than one pot.

Chicken Broth

Easy to Intermediate $3^1/_2$ to $4^1/_2$ hours
Freezes well for 4 to 6 months   Makes about $2^1/_2$ quarts

5 pounds chicken parts, (necks, backs, thighs and wings)

2 medium carrots, unpeeled and cut into chunks

1 medium onion, peeled and halved

3 celery stalks with leaves attached, cut into chunks

$1^1/_2$ teaspoons black peppercorns

1 bay leaf

4 sprigs parsley

4 to 5 quarts water, or enough to cover

1. In a large stockpot, combine the chicken parts, carrots, onion, celery, peppercorns, bay leaf, and parsley. Add the water to cover.

2. Over medium-high heat, bring the liquid to a boil. Skim off any foam. After the liquid boils, reduce the heat to medium-low. Simmer for 3 to 4 hours, skimming the fat and foam every half hour or so. Add additional water if too much has evaporated.

3. Strain the broth and discard the solids. Use immediately or cool, uncovered, by placing the pot in an ice bath and stirring the broth, then refrigerate it for several hours or overnight and remove any solidified fat. Use within 2 to 3 days or freeze.

Turkey Soup: Use turkey parts or a meaty, cut-up, leftover carcass and some of the leftover meat from a holiday meal.

Beef Broth

Many recipes for beef broth require roasted bones and several time-consuming steps. This is an easy beef broth to prepare, and the recipe can be doubled.

For a stronger-tasting chicken or beef broth, just reduce it. Once strained and cooled, and after the fat has been removed, return the broth to a saucepan and simmer over medium heat until the broth is reduced by half. This broth would be excellent in soups, stews, and sauces where you want a richer taste.

Beef Broth

Easy to Intermediate   2 to 2$\frac{1}{2}$ hours
Freezes well for 4 to 6 months   Makes about 2 quarts

2$\frac{1}{2}$ to 3 pounds beef bottom round or rump roast, cut into a few large chunks

2 medium carrots, cut into chunks

1 medium onion, peeled and halved

2 celery stalks with leaves attached, cut into chunks

2 plum tomatoes, halved and seeded

2 sprigs parsley

1 bay leaf

3$\frac{1}{2}$ to 4 quarts water

1. In a large stockpot, combine the beef, carrots, onion, celery, tomatoes, parsley, and bay leaf. Add the water to cover.

2. Over medium-high heat, bring the liquid to a boil. Skim off any foam. When the liquid boils, reduce the heat to medium-low and simmer for 1$\frac{1}{2}$ to 2 hours, skimming the fat and foam every half hour or so. Add additional water if too much has evaporated.

3. Strain the broth, reserve the meat, but discard the remaining solid ingredients. The meat can be sliced and served. Use the broth immediately or cool, uncovered, by placing the pot in an ice bath and stirring the broth, then refrigerate it for several hours or overnight and remove any solidified fat. Use within 2 to 3 days or freeze.

Vegetable Broth

This super, straightforward vegetarian broth is for general use. You can add or substitute other vegetables that you like. The recipe can be doubled. See p. 75 for a richer-flavored Browned Vegetable Broth.

When making a vegetable broth for general use, do not include cauliflower, broccoli, cabbage, turnips, or beets because they will discolor the broth and impart too strong a taste.

Vegetable Broth

Easy   1¹/₂ to 2 hours
Freezes well for 4 to 6 months   Makes about 2 quarts

1 large potato, cut into chunks

2 medium carrots, cut into chunks

1 to 2 small parsnips, cut into chunks

2 celery stalks with leaves attached, cut into chunks

2 medium leeks, washed and cut into chunks

1 medium onion, sliced

1¹/₃ cups mushroom stems (not shiitake), optional

3 sprigs parsley

1 bay leaf

1 teaspoon black peppercorns

2¹/₂ to 3 quarts water

1. In a large stockpot, combine the potato, carrots, parsnips, celery, leeks, onion, mushroom stems, parsley, bay leaf, and peppercorns. Add the water to cover.

2. Over medium-high heat, bring the liquid to a boil. When the liquid boils, reduce the heat to medium-low and simmer 50 to 60 minutes.

3. Strain the broth and press gently on the vegetables in the sieve with the back of a wooden spoon. Discard the solid ingredients. Use the broth immediately or cool, uncovered, by placing the pot in an ice bath and stirring the broth, then refrigerate it. Use within 3 days or freeze.

Mushroom Broth

This full-bodied broth is a natural in mushroom and vegetable soups and for vegetarian versions of legume soups such as split pea or lentil.

With a hearty, almost meaty flavor, this broth can be a replacement for beef or chicken broth in many recipes. When made with water, it is a flavorful vegetarian broth to use as an alternative to vegetable broth.

Mushroom Broth

Easy   30 to 40 minutes
Freezes well up to 4 months   Makes 1 to 1½ quarts

6 cups canned low-sodium chicken broth or water

1 cup chopped mushroom stems (not shiitake stems) or mushrooms

6 to 8 dried mushrooms, such as porcini or shiitake

1 celery stalk, coarsely chopped

1 small carrot, coarsely chopped

1 small onion, peeled and thinly sliced

1. In a medium saucepan over medium heat, combine the broth or water, mushroom stems, dried mushrooms, celery, carrot, and onion. Bring the liquid to a boil and reduce the heat to medium-low so the liquid barely bubbles. Simmer for 20 to 30 minutes.

2. Strain and discard the solids. Use the broth immediately or cool, uncovered, by placing the pot in an ice bath and stirring the broth, then refrigerate. Use within 3 days or freeze.

Fish Broth

This broth is one of the fastest to make. Ask the fishmonger at the market for bones. If you are making a recipe that calls for shrimp, save the shells and use them in the broth (or store them in the freezer until you're ready to make this broth). This recipe can be doubled.

Never boil fish broth or it will become so cloudy and take on such an unappealing taste that it will be ruined for use in soup. If this happens, you'll have to start again.

Fish Broth

Easy to Intermediate   30 to 45 minutes
Freezes well for 2 months   Makes about 1¹/₂ quarts

1¹/₂ pounds fish bones, from mild-flavored fish such as sea bass, cod, grouper, monkfish, sole, snapper, and scrod

1 celery stalk with leaves attached, cut into chunks

1 small onion, peeled and halved

1 leek, washed and cut into chunks

1 bay leaf

1–2 cups shrimp shells, optional

5 to 6 cups water

1 cup dry white wine, vermouth, or additional water

1. In a medium stockpot or Dutch oven, combine the bones, celery, onion, leek, bay leaf, shrimp shells (if you're using them), water and wine to cover.

2. Over medium-high heat, bring the liquid to a gentle boil. Immediately reduce the heat to medium-low so the liquid barely bubbles. Simmer for 20 to 30 minutes.

3. Strain the broth and discard the solid ingredients. Use the broth immediately or cool, uncovered, by placing the pot in an ice bath and stirring the broth; then refrigerate it. Use within 2 days or freeze.

Shrimp Broth

Full of shrimp flavor, this simple broth is not only quick, but is very easy to prepare. It's a fine substitute for fish broth in the soup recipes.

Shrimp Broth

Easy   30 minutes
Do not freeze   Makes 1 to 1½ quarts

6 cups canned low-sodium chicken broth

Shells from ½ to 1 pound shrimp

1 celery stalk, coarsely chopped

1 small carrot, coarsely chopped

1 small onion, peeled and halved

1. In a large saucepan over medium heat, combine the broth, shrimp shells, celery, carrot, and onion. Bring the liquid to a gentle boil and immediately reduce the heat to medium-low so the liquid barely bubbles. Simmer for 20 to 30 minutes.

2. Strain and discard the solids. Use the broth immediately or cool, uncovered, by placing the pot in an ice bath and stirring the broth; then refrigerate it. Use within 2 days or freeze.

Clam Broth

Use this in recipes for clam chowders or as an alternative to fish stock when you're in a hurry.

Clam Broth

Easy   5 minutes   Do not freeze
Makes any amount

Bottled clam juice

Water

1. Combine equal amounts of the clam juice and water to make the amount you need for a recipe, such as 1 cup clam juice and 1 cup water.

Basic Dashi

Dashi is the broth used in most Japanese soups and will impart an authentic taste. The ingredients for making it can be found in Asian or Japanese groceries. You can also purchase instant dashi which can be added to boiling water.

Do not boil the dashi. Don't cover the pot to more quickly return the water to a boil; if you do, the dashi will have an unpleasant taste and become cloudy. You would have to toss out the dashi and start again from scratch.

Basic Dashi

Easy to Intermediate   10 minutes
Do not freeze   Makes 4 to 4½ cups

3- to 4-inch piece dried kelp or kombu   ½ to 1 cup dried bonito fish flakes

4 to 4½ cups cold water

1. Wipe the dried kelp with a damp cloth, taking care not to remove its white powdery coating. With scissors, cut the kelp into several strips.

2. In a medium pot over medium heat, combine 4 cups of the water and the dried kelp. When the water starts to boil, remove the dried kelp with tongs or a slotted spoon and discard.

3. Add the remaining ½ cup cold water and the bonito flakes. When the water returns to a boil, immediately remove the pot from the heat and set aside.

4. After the bonito flakes have sunk to the bottom of the pot, about 3 minutes, strain the dashi through a strainer lined with cheese cloth or through a fine-meshed sieve. Discard the solids and use the broth immediately.

The Least You Need to Know

➤ Homemade broth is the tastiest foundation for soups.

➤ Strain broth through a sieve.

➤ Don't add salt to broth; add salt to the soup you make from it.

➤ Follow instructions on p. 81 for chilling and storing broth safely.

Chapter 14

Garden Variety Soups

In This Chapter

➤ Curried Zucchini Soup

➤ Sweet Potato Soup

➤ Turnip Apple Soup

➤ Spiced Butternut Apple Soup

➤ Thrifty French Housewife's Soup

➤ Herbed Beet Soup

➤ Roasted Red or Yellow Pepper Soup

➤ Fresh Tomato Basil Soup

➤ Savory Tomato-Vegetable Rice Soup

➤ Lettuce and Herb Soup

➤ Parsnip and Blue Cheese Soup

➤ Eggplant and Garlic Soup

➤ Wild Rice and Mushroom Soup

➤ Mushroom Barley Soup

➤ Spring Vegetable Soup

➤ Cabbage and Bacon Soup

➤ Nana's Mix-and-Match Vegetable Soup

When it comes to soup, vegetables—all too often bit players in other dishes—can take top billing. They present an infinite array of appealing combinations and variations. From robust to light, vegetable soups can be served throughout the year, taking advantage of spring and summer's harvest or the hardier bounty of colder weather.

Try to purchase the freshest produce you can. Country farm stalls or city farmers' markets generally carry the cream of the crop, but many large groceries sell high-quality vegetables.

Curried Zucchini Soup

This remarkably easy recipe turns zucchini into a delightfully spiced soup.

This soup is just as tasty served cold. Add the cream, cool, then chill in the refrigerator for $1^1/_2$ to 2 hours, garnish, and serve.

Curried Zucchini Soup

Easy   Food Processor, Blender, or Hand Blender
Prep: 10 minutes; Cooking: 35 to 45 minutes   Freezes well   Serves 6

2 tablespoons butter or margarine

1 small onion, chopped

1 lump clove garlic, minced

2 teaspoons good-quality curry powder, preferably Madras

4 cups chicken or vegetable broth (see p. 106)

2 pounds, about 5 to 6, small zucchini, sliced

Salt to taste (start with $^3/_4$ to 1 teaspoon)

$^1/_2$ cup cream or half-and-half, optional

Fresh chopped mint leaves or chopped chives for garnish

1. In a large pot over medium-low heat, melt the butter. Add the onion and sauté, stirring occasionally, until translucent, about 5 to 7 minutes. Add the garlic and curry powder and sauté, stirring occasionally, for 2 minutes.

2. Add the chicken broth and zucchini. Cover partially and simmer until the zucchini is very tender, about 20 to 25 minutes.

3. Puree the mixture in batches in a food processor or blender. Alternatively, if you have a hand blender, leave the soup in the pot and blend.

4. Taste, season with salt, and stir in the cream if you're using it. Return the mixture to the pot and heat thoroughly over medium heat for about 5 to 10 minutes. Serve garnished with mint or chives.

Sweet Potato Soup

Sweet potatoes, lightly scented with cinnamon and cloves, are the star of this unusual and lovely soup.

Bake extra sweet potatoes when you're already making them and mash them with seasonings as directed. Cover and store the mashed sweet potatoes in the refrigerator. Complete the soup the following day by combining the potatoes with the broth and milk.

Sweet Potato Soup

Easy Prep: 1 hour; Cooking: 10 to 15 minutes
Freezes well   Serves 6 to 8

3 pounds sweet potatoes	$1/4$ teaspoon ground white pepper
2 tablespoons butter	$1/8$ teaspoon ground cloves or allspice
$1/3$ cup orange juice	$2^1/2$ cups chicken broth
2 tablespoons brown sugar	$1/2$ cup milk, half-and-half, or cream
$1/2$ teaspoon cinnamon	Salt to taste

1. Preheat the oven to 400°F. Prick the sweet potatoes with a knife and bake for 50 to 60 minutes or until the potatoes are cooked through and can easily be pierced with a paring knife.

2. Halve the potatoes and scoop out the pulp, discarding the skins. Press the sweet potato pulp through a potato ricer or a food mill into a large bowl, or place the flesh in a large bowl and mash it thoroughly with a potato masher.

3. Add the butter, orange juice, brown sugar, cinnamon, pepper, and ground cloves. Stir until smooth. There should be about 4 cups of mashed sweet potatoes.

4. In a large pot, combine the potatoes, broth, and milk and heat thoroughly over medium heat for about 5 to 10 minutes. Thin with additional juice or milk if necessary. Season with salt. Serve garnished with chives.

Turnip Apple Soup

Turnip soup? Why not! Turnips, mellowed with apples, make one absolutely stunning soup.

Golden Delicious are called for in this recipe, but you can try other sweet apples. Red Delicious, Cortland, and Rome are all excellent substitutes. Rome apples are wonderfully flavorful, but are sometimes almost twice the size of other apples—you might only need one or one and a half of these.

Turnip Apple Soup

Easy—Food Processor or Blender
Prep: 10 to 15 minutes; Cooking: 45 to 55 minutes   Freezes well   Serves 6

$1^1/_4$ pounds white turnips or rutabaga, peeled and cut into $1^1/_2$-inch chunks

2 tablespoons butter

1 small onion, chopped

2 medium Golden Delicious apples, peeled, cored, and chopped

1 tablespoon sugar

$1/_4$ teaspoon cinnamon

$1/_8$ teaspoon freshly grated nutmeg

3 cups chicken broth

$1/_2$ cup half-and-half, milk, or apple cider

Salt to taste, about $3/_4$ teaspoon

1. Put the turnips in a large saucepan and cover them with plenty of cold water. Over medium-high heat, bring the water to a boil and boil the turnips until they can be pierced easily with a fork and are very tender, about 10 to 15 minutes. Drain well in a colander.

2. Meanwhile, in a small skillet over medium heat, melt the butter. Add the onion and apples and sauté, stirring occasionally, until very tender, about 10 to 15 minutes. Add the sugar, cinnamon, and nutmeg and cook, stirring occasionally, for 5 minutes.

3. Puree the turnips and apple-onion mixture in a food processor or blender until smooth. Add a little broth, if necessary.

4. Transfer the puree to a large pot. Add the chicken broth, half-and-half, and salt to taste. Heat over medium heat until hot, about 10 minutes. Thin with extra broth, if necessary, when reheating.

Spiced Butternut Apple Soup

A fall and winter classic in my kitchen, this warming soup is a delightful blend of butternut squash, apples, cinnamon, and curry.

Souper Bowl Fact

Butternut and other winter squash, such as acorn and Hubbard, are good sources of vitamins A and C as well as iron. Feel free to try other winter squash in this soup.

Spiced Butternut Apple Soup

Easy   Food Processor, Blender, or Hand Blender
Prep: 10 to 15; Cooking: 40 to 45 minutes   Freezes well   Serves 6

2 tablespoons butter or margarine

2 medium onions, chopped

1 cinnamon stick

1 bay leaf

1^1/$_2$ tablespoons good-quality curry powder, preferably Madras

3 cups chicken or vegetable broth

1^3/$_4$ pounds butternut squash, peeled, seeded and cut into 1^1/$_2$- inch chunks, about 3^1/$_2$ to 4 cups

2 medium Granny Smith apples, peeled, cored, and chopped

^{3}/$_4$ cup apple cider or apple juice

Salt to taste, about ^{3}/$_4$ to 1 teaspoon

1. In a large pot over medium-low heat, melt the butter. Add the onions, cinnamon stick, and bay leaf and sauté, stirring often, until translucent, about 5 to 7 minutes. Add the curry powder and cook, stirring often, for 2 minutes.

2. Add the chicken broth, butternut, and apples and simmer, partially covered, until tender, about 20 to 25 minutes. Remove the bay leaf and cinnamon stick.

3. With a slotted spoon, transfer the butternut, apples, and onions to a food processor, but leave the broth in the pot. Puree until smooth. Alternatively, if you have a hand blender, leave the soup in the pot and blend.

4. Return the puree to the pot. Add the apple cider and salt, and stir to blend. Heat thoroughly over medium heat for 5 to 10 minutes. If the soup is too thick, thin with extra apple cider.

Thrifty French Housewife's Soup

Traditionally named for women who are noted for their skill and frugality in the kitchen, other titles for this recipe could be "Nothing's In The Fridge Soup" or "Don't Get Paid 'Til Friday Soup." It's cheap, easy, and always good.

Add a few leftover cooked vegetables such as green beans, peas, or broccoli in step 2. You'll need to thin the soup with additional broth.

Thrifty French Housewife's Soup

Easy   Food Processor, Blender, or Hand Blender
Prep: 10 to 15 minutes; Cooking: 55 to 65 minutes   Freezes well   Serves 6

3 tablespoons butter or margarine

2 medium onions, thinly sliced

2 celery stalks, chopped

l large or 2 medium carrots, chopped

$1/2$ teaspoon minced fresh thyme leaves or $1/4$ teaspoon dried

5 cups chicken or vegetable broth

$3/4$ pounds potatoes, about 2 medium, peeled and thinly sliced

$1/2$ cup chopped parsley

Salt to taste, about $1/2$ to $3/4$ teaspoon

Freshly ground black pepper

1. In a large pot over medium heat, melt the butter. Add the onion, celery, carrot, and thyme and sauté, stirring occasionally, until softened, about 10 to 15 minutes.

2. Add the chicken broth, potatoes, and parsley. Cook, partially covered, until the vegetables are very tender, 35 to 45 minutes.

3. Puree in batches in a food processor or blender until smooth. Alternatively, if you have a hand blender, leave the soup in the pot and blend.

4. Return the soup to the pot. Thin with additional broth, water, or milk if necessary. Taste, and season with salt and pepper. Heat thoroughly over medium heat about 5 to 10 minutes.

Herbed Beet Soup

A variation of borscht, this smooth ruby-colored soup is truly a masterpiece. It can be made with fresh cooked or canned beets and is excellent hot or cold.

This soup can also be served cold. After pureeing, chill thoroughly, about 1¹/₂ to 2 hours. Garnish and serve.

Herbed Beet Soup

Easy   Food Processor, Blender, or Hand Blender
Prep: 10 minutes, plus 35 to 45 minutes beet-cooking time; Cooking: 30 to 35 minutes
Freezes well   Serves 4 to 6

2 tablespoons butter or margarine

1 medium onion, chopped

1¹/₂ tablespoons all-purpose flour

3 cups chicken broth

1 pound (3–4 medium) beets, cooked, skinned, and sliced, (or 2¹/₂ to 3 cups canned beets, drained)

1 teaspoon minced fresh thyme or ¹/₂ teaspoon dried

³/₄ teaspoon minced fresh rosemary or ¹/₄ teaspoon dried

1¹/₂ teaspoons red wine vinegar or lemon juice

¹/₂ teaspoon Dijon mustard

Salt to taste

¹/₂ cup sour cream, nonfat sour cream, or yogurt for garnish

Chopped fresh chives or snipped fresh dill for garnish

1. In a large pot over medium-low heat, melt the butter. Add the onion and sauté, stirring occasionally, until translucent, about 5 minutes.

2. Add the flour and cook, stirring constantly, for 3 to 5 minutes. Add the chicken broth.

3. Increase the heat to medium and cook until the broth thickens slightly, about 5 minutes.

4. Add the cooked beets, thyme, rosemary, wine vinegar, and mustard. Simmer, partially covered, for 10 to 15 minutes.

5. Puree in batches in a food processor or blender until smooth. Alternatively, if you have a hand blender, leave the soup in the pot and blend.

6. Return the soup to the pot. Thin with additional broth if necessary. Reduce the heat to medium-low and reheat thoroughly. Taste, and season with salt. Serve garnished with sour cream and chives.

Roasted Red or Yellow Pepper Soup

Roasted bell peppers make a splendid soup. Roasting not only removes the skin, but it also softens the flesh and intensifies the sweetness of the peppers while adding a smoky undertone.

Roasted Red or Yellow Pepper Soup

Intermediate to Challenging   Food Processor, Blender, or Hand Blender
Prep: 30 minutes; Cooking: 60 minutes   Freezes well   Serves 4 to 6

6 medium red or yellow bell peppers, seeded and halved

2 tablespoons olive oil, plus additional for rubbing the peppers

1 medium onion, chopped

1 small celery stalk, finely diced, about $1/3$ cup

2 cups shredded carrots, about 3 to 4 medium

1 plump clove garlic, minced

$2/3$ cup dry white wine or vermouth

$3^1/2$ cups chicken or vegetable broth

$1^1/2$ teaspoons chopped fresh rosemary or $3/4$ teaspoon dried

Salt to taste, about $1/2$ to $3/4$ teaspoon

$1/4$ teaspoon freshly ground black pepper

$1/8$ teaspoon cayenne, optional

2 teaspoons fresh lemon juice

$1/4$ cup sour cream, nonfat sour cream, or light cream for garnish, optional

1. **To roast the peppers:** Preheat the broiler. Flatten the peppers slightly. Lightly rub them with some olive oil, put them skin side up on a broiler tray or baking sheet, and broil until the skins are blistered and charred. Put the peppers in a paper or plastic bag and close tightly. When the peppers are cool enough to handle, peel, using a paring knife to help scrape off and discard the skin. Slice the peppers thinly. (This step can be done in advance.)

2. In a large pot over medium heat, heat the olive oil. Add the onion and celery. Sauté, stirring occasionally, until very tender, about 15 minutes. Add the carrots and garlic and sauté, stirring occasionally, for 5 minutes. Add the white wine and cook for 3 minutes.

3. Add the broth, peppers, and rosemary. Reduce the heat to medium-low. Cover and simmer until the vegetables are very tender, about 30 minutes.

4. Strain the soup, reserving the broth. Puree the vegetables with a small amount of the broth in batches in a food processor or blender until smooth. Alternatively, if you have a hand blender, leave the soup in the pot and blend.

5. Combine the puree with enough of the reserved broth to make the desired consistency. Season with salt, pepper, cayenne, and lemon juice. Reheat over medium heat. Swirl in the cream or sour cream if you like.

Fresh Tomato Basil Soup

Tomato and basil are perfect partners in everything, not least in this superb soup. This soup is best in the summer when tomatoes are at their peak. During winter months, use plum tomatoes or costly ripe, imported tomatoes.

Fresh Tomato Basil Soup

Easy   Food Processor, Blender, or Hand Blender
Prep: 15 minutes; Cooking: 40 minutes   Freezes well   Serves 4 to 6

2 tablespoons olive oil	1 cup vegetable or chicken broth
1 medium onion, chopped	Salt to taste, about $1/2$ to 1 teaspoon
1 plump clove garlic, minced	$1/4$ teaspoon freshly ground black pepper
$3^1/2$ pounds ripe, fresh tomatoes, peeled, seeded, and coarsely chopped with juices	2 tablespoons minced fresh basil or prepared pesto
$1/2$ bay leaf	

1. In a large pot over medium heat, heat the olive oil. Add the onion and sauté, stirring occasionally, until the onion is tender and golden, about 10 minutes. Add the garlic and cook, stirring, for 1 minute.

2. Add the tomatoes and bay leaf, then cover and simmer until the tomatoes are very soft, about 30 minutes.

3. Remove the bay leaf. Puree in batches in a food processor until smooth. Alternatively, if you have a hand blender, leave the soup in the pot and blend.

4. Return the soup to the pot. Add the broth and reheat until hot. Season with salt and pepper. Stir in the basil or pesto before serving.

Souper Bowl Fact

Tomatoes originated in South America and were transported from the New World to Europe by the Spanish. The French, believing this fruit of the vine was an aphrodisiac, called them *pommes d'amour,* or love apples.

Savory Tomato-Vegetable Rice Soup

This herb-infused tomato-based soup, accented by vegetables and rice, is a pleasing alternative to broth-based vegetable soups.

Substitute other vegetables such as diced yellow squash and sliced green beans for the zucchini and peas.

Savory Tomato-Vegetable Rice Soup

Easy to Intermediate   Prep: 10 to 15 minutes; Cooking: 50 to 60 minutes
Freezes well   Serves 6 to 8

For the Bouquet Garni:

1 bay leaf

2 small to medium sprigs fresh thyme (or $1/2$ teaspoon dried thyme)

3 to 4 sprigs parsley

3 black peppercorns

2 whole cloves

For the Soup:

2 tablespoons olive oil

1 medium onion, chopped

1 small carrot, finely diced

1 small celery stalk, finely diced

$3^1/2$ cups chicken broth

$2^1/2$ cups fresh or canned tomato puree

$1/4$ cup white rice

1 medium zucchini or 2 baby zucchini, cut into half moons

3 to 4 teaspoons sugar, or to taste

$2/3$ cup frozen or fresh peas

Salt to taste, about $1/2$ to 1 teaspoon

$1/4$ teaspoon freshly ground black pepper, or to taste

2 tablespoons chopped fresh flat-leaf parsley

1. Prepare the bouquet garni by wrapping the ingredients in a small piece of cheesecloth and tying it to secure. Set aside.

2. In a large pot over medium-low heat, heat the olive oil. Add the onion, carrot, and celery, and sauté, stirring occasionally, until tender, about 15 minutes.

3. Add the broth, tomato puree, rice, zucchini, sugar, and bouquet garni. Cover partially and simmer for 30 to 35 minutes. Add the peas and simmer, uncovered, for 5 to 10 minutes until the peas are cooked through.

4. Remove the bouquet garni and discard. Season with salt and pepper. Stir in the parsley.

Lettuce and Herb Soup

I prefer to use romaine in this soup, but feel free to try other green lettuce varieties— anything except iceberg, which is too watery and flavorless.

Lettuce and Herb Soup

Intermediate

Food Processor, Blender, or Hand Blender   Prep: 10 minutes; Cooking: 15 minutes
Freezes well   Serves 4 to 6

1 tablespoon butter or margarine	$1^{1}/_{3}$ cups half-and-half or milk
6 scallions, white part only, thinly sliced	1 egg yolk
3 cups vegetable or chicken broth	Salt to taste, about $^{1}/_{2}$ to $^{3}/_{4}$ teaspoon
8 cups chopped romaine lettuce	Freshly ground black pepper
2 tablespoons chopped parsley	Freshly grated Romano or Parmesan cheese for garnish, optional
2 tablespoons minced fresh herbs: any combination of basil, chervil, thyme, chives, or celery leaves	

1. In a large pot over medium heat, melt the butter. Add the scallions and sauté, stirring occasionally, until softened, about 3 minutes.

2. Add the broth and bring to a boil. Add the lettuce, cover, and simmer until the lettuce is wilted, about 3 to 5 minutes.

3. Add the parsley and mixed herbs. Puree the mixture in batches in a food processor or blender. Alternatively, if you have a hand blender, leave the soup in the pot and blend.

4. Return the mixture to the pot and reheat over medium-low heat.

5. In a small bowl, lightly whisk together the half-and-half and egg yolk. While whisking constantly, add a little heated soup to the egg mixture. While whisking constantly, pour the egg mixture into the soup in a steady stream. Simmer gently over medium-low heat until the soup thickens slightly. Do not let the soup boil. Season with salt and freshly ground black pepper. Serve with Romano cheese on the side.

Souper Bowl Fact

Romaine, also known as Cos lettuce, is reportedly native to the island of Cos in the Aegean Sea. This crisp and flavorful green is the primary ingredient in the ever-popular Caesar Salad.

Parsnip and Blue Cheese Soup

Parsnips can hold their own in the presence of strong-flavored blue cheese, and the two blend harmoniously in this unique soup.

Parsnips and carrots are perfect companions. For a colorful variation, use $1/2$ pound parsnips and $1/2$ pound carrots in this soup.

Parsnip and Blue Cheese Soup

Intermediate   Food Processor, Blender, or Hand Blender
Prep: 15 minutes; Cooking: 40 to 45 minutes   Do not freeze   Serves 6

For the Bouquet Garni:

1 bay leaf

2 whole cloves

1 sprig of thyme

3 parsley stems

For the Soup:

2 tablespoons butter or margarine

1 medium onion, chopped

1 plump clove garlic, minced

$4^1/2$ cups chicken or vegetable broth

1 pound parsnips, peeled and diced, woody cores removed

1 medium potato, about 8 ounces, diced

$1^1/2$ cups half-and-half, cream, or milk

$1/2$ cup crumbled blue cheese

$1/4$ cup freshly ground Parmesan cheese

2 tablespoons chopped chives

1. Prepare the bouquet garni by wrapping the ingredients in a small piece of cheesecloth and tying it to secure. Set aside.

2. In a large pot over medium heat, melt the butter. Add the onion and sauté, stirring occasionally, until translucent, about 5 minutes. Add the garlic and cook, stirring often, for 1 to 2 minutes.

3. Add the broth, parsnips, potatoes, and bouquet garni. Bring the liquid to a boil. Reduce the heat to medium-low. Cover and simmer until tender, about 30 to 35 minutes. Remove the bouquet garni and discard.

4. Use a slotted spoon to lift the solids into a bowl, leaving the broth in the pot. In a food processor or blender, puree the vegetables in batches with a small amount of the broth, until smooth, returning each pureed batch to the pot. Alternatively, if you have a hand blender, leave the soup in the pot and blend.

5. Return all the puree to the pot and reheat over medium-low heat. The soup can be made ahead to this point.

6. In a small saucepan over medium-low heat, heat the half-and-half. Add the blue cheese and Parmesan, stirring constantly, until the cheese is melted.

7. Stir the cheese mixture into the soup. Thin, if necessary, with extra broth or half-and-half. Serve immediately, garnished with chopped chives. To reheat this soup, do so over medium-low heat, stirring frequently.

Eggplant and Garlic Soup

Eggplant, enhanced by garlic, is transformed into an elegant, smooth soup. It's excellent as a light meal or starter.

Eggplant and Garlic Soup

Easy   Food Processor, Blender, or Hand Blender
Prep: 10 to 15 minutes; Cooking: 50 to 60 minutes   Freezes well   Serves 6

3 tablespoons olive oil

1 medium onion, chopped

1¼ pounds eggplant, peeled and diced

6 plump cloves garlic, minced—about 1 tablespoon

½ teaspoon ground cumin

½ teaspoon turmeric

4 cups vegetable or chicken broth

1 small potato, peeled and diced

Salt to taste, about ¾ teaspoon

¼ teaspoon freshly ground white pepper

¼ teaspoon ground cayenne

Fresh chopped cilantro for garnish

1. In a large pot over medium heat, heat 1 tablespoon of the olive oil. Add the onion and sauté, stirring occasionally, until translucent, about 5 minutes.

2. Add the remaining 2 tablespoons of olive oil and heat. Add the eggplant, garlic, cumin, and turmeric. Sauté, stirring occasionally, until softened, about 5 to 7 minutes.

3. Add the broth and potato. Reduce the heat to medium-low. Cover and simmer until the vegetables are very tender, about 30 to 40 minutes.

4. Puree in batches in a food processor or blender until smooth. Alternatively, if you have a hand blender, leave the soup in the pot and blend.

5. Reheat over medium heat, stirring occasionally. Thin with additional broth if necessary. Season with salt, white pepper, and cayenne. Garnish with cilantro.

Souper Bowl Fact

Eggplants, like tomatoes, belong to the nightshade family and are not actually classified as a vegetable, but rather as another fruit of the vine. Garlic has been the subject of much folklore. Throughout the ages, the pungent bulb has been credited not only with magical and mystical powers to ward off vampires and evil spirits, but also with many health-giving properties. Its proponents claim that eating it promotes strength, longevity, and a healthy heart. It has also been billed as a remedy for the common cold and toothaches.

Wild Rice and Mushroom Soup

The nutty taste of wild rice is outstanding with mushrooms. Try to include some wild mushrooms such as shiitakes (without their woody stems, please!), which are readily available fresh in many supermarkets.

For extra mushroom flavor, soak 5 to 6 wild mushrooms in 1 cup of boiling water for 20 minutes. Strain the liquid through a sieve lined with a coffee filter. Chop the mushrooms coarsely and set aside. Replace part of the broth with the mushroom-soaking liquid and add these mushrooms with the broth.

Wild Rice and Mushroom Soup

Easy   Prep: 10 minutes; Cooking: 70 to 80 minutes
Freezes well   Serves 6 to 8

$^1/_2$ cup wild or brown rice

2 tablespoons vegetable oil

6 scallions, white part only, minced

1 medium carrot, finely diced

1 stalk celery, finely diced (reserve 1 tablespoon minced celery leaves)

$^3/_4$ pound white, cremini, or shiitake mushrooms or a combination, coarsely chopped

1 teaspoon minced fresh thyme leaves or $^1/_2$ teaspoon dried

3 to 4 tablespoons dry sherry

6 cups chicken or vegetable broth

Salt to taste, about $^1/_2$ to $^3/_4$ teaspoon

$^1/_4$ teaspoon freshly ground black pepper

2 tablespoons minced fresh parsley or chives

$^1/_4$ to $^1/_2$ cup cream, optional

1. Put the rice in a sieve and wash it under cold running water.

2. In a large pot over medium heat, heat the vegetable oil. Add the scallions, carrot, and celery and sauté, stirring occasionally, until tender, about 10 minutes. Add the mushrooms and thyme and cook, stirring occasionally, for 5 minutes.

3. Add the sherry and cook for 1 to 2 minutes. Add the broth and rice. Cover partially and simmer until the rice is tender, 50 to 60 minutes.

4. Season with salt and pepper and stir in the reserved celery leaves and parsley. If you like a richer texture, add the cream.

Mushroom Barley Soup: In winter, this hearty soup is a standard on many home and restaurant menus. Prepare Wild Rice and Mushroom Soup, using white or cremini mushrooms. Substitute $^1/_3$ cup pearl barley for the wild rice. Substitute 1 medium onion, chopped, for the scallions.

Souper Bowl Fact

Early settlers believed that the seed of a long grain marsh grass, native to the northern Great Lakes region, resembled rice and accordingly named it wild rice. Traditionally harvested by Native Americans, now it is also being produced commercially. It can be expensive. If it's beyond your budget, use equal parts of wild and brown rice.

Spring Vegetable Rice Soup

After a long winter, I love this especially light and fresh-tasting soup that hints of spring's arrival.

To make an even heartier meal, add 1 cup cooked chicken or turkey, shredded or diced, when you add the squash and other vegetables.

Spring Vegetable Rice Soup

Easy   Prep: 15 minutes; Cooking: 35 to 40 minutes
Freezes well   Serves 6 to 8

2 tablespoon olive oil

6 scallions, white part only, sliced

1 small carrot, shredded

1 small celery stalk, thinly sliced

1 plump clove garlic, minced

3 to 4 mushrooms, sliced

6 cups chicken or vegetable broth

$1/3$ cup white rice

1 medium tomato, peeled, seeded, and diced

1 small yellow squash, sliced

1 small zucchini, sliced

$1/2$ medium red or yellow bell pepper, cut into thin 1-inch long strips, about $1/2$ cup

$1/4$ pound asparagus, trimmed and sliced (or $1/2$ cup sliced fresh green beans)

3 tablespoons chopped fresh parsley

1 tablespoon minced fresh basil, dill, or chives

Salt to taste, about $1/2$ teaspoon

Freshly ground black pepper to taste

continues

continued

1. In a large pot over medium heat, heat the olive oil. Add the scallions, carrot, and celery and sauté, stirring often, until the vegetables begin to soften, about 5 minutes. Add the garlic and mushrooms and cook, stirring, for 2 minutes.

2. Add the broth, rice, and tomato. Bring the broth to a boil. Reduce the heat to medium-low, cover, and cook until the rice is tender, about 15 to 20 minutes.

3. Add the yellow squash, zucchini, bell pepper, and asparagus and cook, uncovered, until the vegetables are tender, about 7 to 10 minutes. Stir in the parsley and basil and season with salt and pepper.

Cabbage and Bacon Soup

I like to make this soup in late autumn after the first frost, which causes cabbage to acquire a sweeter taste. I add a touch of caraway, but omit it if you want.

To prepare the cabbage for this soup, remove any wilted outer leaves, cut out and discard the tough core, and cut the cabbage into wedges. Slice into thin strips. Refrigerate unused wedges.

Cabbage and Bacon Soup

Easy   Prep: 15 minutes; Cooking: 50 to 60 minutes
Freezes well   Serves 6 to 8

6 strips bacon, sliced into small pieces or strips

2 tablespoons olive oil

1 medium onion, halved and thinly sliced

5$^1/_2$ cups cabbage

7 cups chicken broth

1 medium potato, peeled and diced

$^1/_4$ to $^1/_2$ teaspoon caraway seeds, optional

Salt to taste, about $^1/_2$ to $^3/_4$ teaspoon

$^1/_4$ teaspoon freshly ground black pepper

$^1/_4$ cup minced fresh parsley

1. In a skillet, cook the bacon over medium-low heat until most of the fat is rendered. Remove the bacon with a slotted spoon and blot on a paper towel. Set aside.

2. In a large pot over medium-low heat, heat the olive oil. Add the onion and sauté, stirring occasionally, until the onion is almost golden, about 10 minutes. Add the bacon and cook for 5 minutes longer. Add the cabbage and cook, stirring occasionally, for 5 minutes.

3. Add the broth, potato, and caraway. Cover and simmer until the cabbage is very tender, 35 to 40 minutes. Season with salt and pepper. Stir in the parsley and serve immediately.

Nana's Mix-and-Match Vegetable Soup

This is the old-fashioned vegetable soup that grandmothers used to make. Change it according to your mood, what's in season, and what you have on hand. Use the vegetables listed below, or any combination you like, except beets and red cabbage, which are too dominant in flavor and color to blend well in this soup.

This soup is an idea way to use last night's vegetables. Reduce the cooking time by a few minutes if you are using leftovers.

Nana's Mix-and-Match Vegetable Soup

Easy   Prep: 15 to 20 minutes; Cooking: 35 to 40 minutes
Freezes well   Serves 6 to 8

2 tablespoons vegetable or olive oil

1 medium onion, quartered and thinly sliced

1 medium carrot, diced

1 celery stalk, diced (reserve 1 tablespoon chopped leaves)

1 plump clove garlic, minced, optional

6 cups chicken, beef, or vegetable broth

Use a total of 2^1/$_2$ to 3 cups of vegetables from these lists:

Root Veggie Choices:

^{1}/$_2$ cup chopped turnip or rutabaga

^{1}/$_2$ cup diced, peeled potato

^{1}/$_2$ cup diced sweet potato, about 3-ounce potato

Veggie Choices:

^{1}/$_2$ cup fresh or frozen corn kernels

^{1}/$_2$ cup fresh or frozen peas

^{1}/$_2$ cup fresh or frozen string beans

^{1}/$_2$ cup chopped green or savoy cabbage

^{1}/$_2$ cup diced zucchini

^{1}/$_2$ cup diced yellow squash

^{1}/$_2$ cup drained, canned tomatoes, chopped or stewed

Salt to taste, about ^{1}/$_2$ to ^{3}/$_4$ teaspoon

Freshly ground black pepper to taste

2 tablespoons minced fresh parsley

1. In a large pot over medium heat, heat the vegetable oil. Add the onion, carrot, and celery and sauté, stirring occasionally, until softened, about 10 minutes. Add the garlic and cook, stirring, for 1 minute.

2. Add the broth and any selections from the root veggies list. Cover and bring the liquid to a gentle boil. Once it has boiled, cover partially and simmer until the vegetables are almost tender, about 10 to 15 minutes.

3. Add your choices from the veggie choices list. Add additional broth if you want to add more veggies than suggested or if the soup is too chunky for you. Simmer, uncovered, until the vegetables are tender, about 10 to 12 minutes.

4. Season with salt and pepper. Stir in the parsley and reserved celery leaves.

The Least You Need to Know

➤ Vegetable soups take advantage of summer and winter produce.

➤ Buy good-quality fresh produce.

➤ Vegetables can be left whole for a chunky texture or pureed for a smoother texture.

➤ Leftover vegetables can be used in pureed soup.

Energetic
Pea Soup

Chapter 15

Legume Soups

In this Chapter

➤ Yellow Pea Soup

➤ Old Fashioned Split Pea Soup

➤ Spicy Peanut Soup

➤ Vegetarian Lentil Soup

➤ Lentil Soup with Sausage and Potatoes

➤ South of the Border Black Bean Soup

➤ Garlicky White Bean Soup

➤ Chickpea and Sausage Soup

➤ Poor Man's Pinto Bean Soup

Not a vegetable, legumes are actually pod-ripened seeds with more culinary virtues than many other foods. There are thousands of varieties, but the most well-known are beans, lentils, peas, and peanuts. With a high nutritional value, legumes are a dietary staple throughout the world. Some, such as soybeans, are high in protein, and most are high in fiber and carbohydrates, and are a remarkably rich source of B vitamins and minerals such as iron and calcium. Best of all, legumes can easily be transformed into marvelous, filling soups that generally freeze well. Sometimes legume soups get too thick during cooking or after storing, but a little extra water or broth will restore them to the right consistency.

Yellow Pea Soup

A hint of garlic, thyme, and mustard pep up this warming soup. For a vegetarian version, omit the ham hock.

Yellow Pea Soup

Easy   Food Processor, Blender, or Hand Blender
Prep: 30 minutes; Cooking: 1½ to 2 hours   Freezes well   Serves 6 to 8

1 pound dried yellow split peas, rinsed and picked over

8 cups water

1 small ham hock, optional

2 medium onions, chopped

1 large carrot, peeled and chopped

2 plump cloves garlic, minced

3 tablespoons minced fresh parsley

1½ teaspoons minced fresh thyme or ¾ teaspoon dried

1¼ teaspoons prepared Dijon mustard

Salt to taste, about ½ to 1 teaspoon

½ teaspoon freshly ground black pepper, or to taste

1. In a large pot over medium heat, combine the yellow split peas, water, and ham hock. Cover and bring the water to a boil. Simmer, uncovered, for 15 minutes. Skim off any foam that forms. Reduce the heat to medium-low.

2. Add the onions, carrot, garlic, parsley, thyme, and mustard. Simmer, partially covered, until the peas and ham are very tender, about 1 to 1½ hours.

3. Remove the ham and chop the meat, discarding the bone. Set the meat aside.

4. Puree the soup in batches in a food processor or blender. Alternatively, if you have a hand blender, leave the soup in the pot and blend.

5. Season with salt and pepper to taste. Return the ham to the soup and reheat.

Souper Bowl Fact

Yellow split pea soup hails from both Canada and Scandinavia, whereas green split pea soup is a Dutch treat.

Old-Fashioned Split Pea Soup

This traditional winter soup should be thick as a heavy fog. Some people don't like to puree the soup, but simply simmer it a bit longer until it cooks down to the right consistency.

Old-Fashioned Split Pea Soup

Easy   Food Processor, Blender, or Hand Blender
Prep: 30 minutes; Cooking: 1^1/$_2$ to 2 hours   Freezes well   Serves 6 to 8

1 pound dried split green peas, rinsed and picked over

8 cups water

1 small ham hock, optional

2 medium onions, chopped

2 medium carrots, peeled and chopped

1 large celery stalk, chopped

1 to 2 plump cloves garlic, minced

^{1}/$_4$ cup chopped parsley

1^1/$_2$ teaspoons minced fresh thyme, or ^{1}/$_2$ teaspoon dried

1 bay leaf

Salt to taste, about ^{1}/$_2$ to 1 teaspoon

^{3}/$_4$ teaspoon freshly ground black pepper, or to taste

Croutons for garnish, optional

1. In a large pot over medium heat, combine the green split peas, water, and ham hock. Cover and bring the water to a boil. Simmer, uncovered, for 15 minutes. Skim off any foam that forms. Reduce the heat to medium-low.

2. Add the onions, carrot, celery, garlic, parsley, thyme, and bay leaf. Simmer, partially covered, until the peas and ham are very tender, about 1 to 1^1/$_2$ hours.

3. Remove the bay leaf and discard. Remove the ham and chop the meat, discarding the bone. Set the meat aside.

4. Puree the soup in batches in a food processor or blender. Alternatively, if you have a hand blender, leave the soup in the pot and blend. Return the ham to the soup, if desired.

5. Season with salt and pepper to taste and reheat. Garnish with homemade or packaged croutons.

Souper Bowl Fact

Both green and yellow split peas are a type of field pea and are specifically grown to be dried (and turned into soup!). They are cousins of the common green garden pea that we eat fresh.

Spicy Peanut Soup

Peanuts, a legume known as "goobers" or "gooberpeas" in some areas of the deep South and "groundnuts" in Africa, are the basis for this velvety soup that graced Colonial tables from Georgia to Virginia. Versions of this soup can also be found throughout West Africa. For a tasty twist, substitute unsweetened coconut milk for the half-and-half.

Spicy Peanut Soup

Easy   Prep: 10 minutes; Cooking: 25 minutes
Do not freeze   Serves 6

2 tablespoons vegetable oil

6 scallions, white part only, chopped; reserve chopped greens from 3 scallions for garnish

1 medium celery stalk, chopped

2 teaspoons minced fresh ginger, about $1/2$-inch piece

$1^1/2$ tablespoons all-purpose flour

4 cups chicken broth

1 cup smooth, natural peanut butter

$1/2$ cup half-and-half or unsweetened coconut milk

$1/2$ to $3/4$ teaspoon cayenne

Salt to taste, about $1/2$ teaspoon

Chopped dry-roasted peanuts for garnish

1. In a large pot over medium heat, heat the vegetable oil. Add the scallions and celery and sauté, stirring occasionally, until softened, about 5 minutes. Add the ginger and cook for 2 minutes, stirring occasionally.

2. Add the flour and cook, stirring frequently, for 3 to 5 minutes.

3. Add the chicken broth and simmer until the broth is hot and slightly thickened, about 5 minutes. For a velvety texture, strain the solids and return the liquid to the pot.

4. Reduce the heat to medium-low. Add the peanut butter, half-and-half, and cayenne, and stir well to blend. Simmer until the soup is heated through, about 5 to 7 minutes. Do not let the soup boil.

5. Season with salt to taste. Serve garnished with peanuts and the reserved scallion greens.

Souper Bowl Fact

Natural peanut butter, although sold commercially, can be made in a food processor by pureeing raw or roasted peanuts, preferably unsalted, with a little peanut oil until they turn into a smooth paste. If you use unsalted peanut butter in the soup, add salt to taste.

Vegetarian Lentil Soup

This savory lentil soup, based on an Italian recipe, has been on my winter menu for lunch or supper for many years. I like this lentil soup without meat, but you can add a small ham hock or ham bone when you add the water. Before pureeing the soup, remove the ham hock and chop and reserve its meat. Add the chopped ham to the pureed soup before reheating. You could also garnish the vegetarian version with a drizzle of red wine vinegar or, for a nonvegetarian dish, sprinkle the vegetarian version with homemade bacon bits.

Vegetarian Lentil Soup

Easy   Food Processor, Blender, or Hand Blender
Prep: 10 minutes; Cooking: 40 to 55 minutes   Freezes well   Serves 8 to 10

2 tablespoons olive oil

2 medium carrots, peeled and chopped

2 medium celery stalks, chopped

1 medium onion, chopped

2 plump cloves garlic, minced

8 cups water

1 pound brown lentils, rinsed and picked over

One 14-ounce can chopped tomatoes, with their juices

2 tablespoons chopped fresh flat-leaf parsley

1 bay leaf

2 teaspoons minced fresh thyme, or 1 teaspoon dried

Salt to taste, about 1 to 1$^1/_2$ teaspoons

$^3/_4$ teaspoon black pepper, or to taste

Freshly ground Parmesan cheese for garnish, optional

1. In a large pot over medium-low heat, heat the olive oil. Add the carrots, celery, and onion and sauté, stirring occasionally, until softened, about 7 minutes. Add the garlic and cook, stirring often, for 2 minutes.

2. Increase the heat to medium. Add the water, lentils, tomatoes, parsley, bay leaf, and thyme. Cover and bring the liquid to a boil.

3. Reduce the heat to medium-low. Simmer, partially covered, until the lentils are tender, about 35 to 45 minutes. Remove the bay leaf.

4. Puree in batches in a food processor or blender. Alternatively, if you have a hand blender, leave the soup in the pot and blend.

5. Season with salt and pepper to taste and reheat. Serve with grated Parmesan cheese on the side if you want.

Lentil Soup with Sausage and Potatoes

Legumes, vegetables, meat, and potatoes, this all-star soup's got everything—great taste, great body, and it's marvelously filling.

Cured, smoked, and salted meats, such as bacon, ham, ham hocks, or sausage, add a salty flavor to the soup when it is cooking. Take extra care when adding salt after the soup is finished.

Lentil Soup with Sausage and Potatoes

Easy   Prep: 10 minutes; Cooking: 55 to 65 minutes   Freezes well   Serves 8 to 10

2 tablespoons olive oil

1 medium celery stalk, chopped

1 medium onion, chopped

1 carrot, chopped

2 plump cloves garlic, minced

8 cups water

1 pound brown lentils, rinsed and picked over

2 medium potatoes, about 12 ounces, peeled and diced

3 tablespoons minced fresh parsley

1 bay leaf

1 teaspoon minced fresh oregano, or $1/2$ teaspoon dried

1 teaspoon minced fresh thyme, or $1/2$ teaspoon dried

4 to 6 ounces sausage, such as kielbasa or chorizo, sliced

Salt to taste, about $1/2$ to 1 teaspoon

$1/2$ teaspoon black pepper

1. In a large pot over medium-low heat, heat the olive oil. Add the celery, onion, and carrot and sauté, stirring occasionally, until softened, about 10 minutes. Add the garlic and cook, stirring often, for 2 minutes.

2. Increase the heat to medium. Add the water, lentils, potatoes, parsley, bay leaf, oregano, and thyme. Cover and bring the liquid to a boil.

3. Reduce the heat to medium-low. Simmer, partially covered, until the potatoes and lentils are tender, about 35 to 45 minutes.

4. Remove the bay leaf. If you want a thicker soup, puree 2 cups of the mixture in a food processor or blender. Return the puree to the pot.

5. Add the sliced sausage and cook for 10 minutes. Season with salt and pepper.

South of the Border Black Bean Soup

This popular black bean soup has many versions throughout Latin America and the Caribbean, particularly in Mexico, Cuba, and Brazil. Spicy and filling, this vegetarian rendition is a hit no matter what the weather.

For an even heartier soup, add $1/4$ to $1/3$ pound sliced chorizo or andouille sausage to the soup after you add the sherry. Serve this version over rice.

South of the Border Black Bean Soup

Easy   Food Processor or Blender
Soaking: 2 hours to overnight; Prep: 15 minutes; Cooking: 2$1/4$ to 3 hours
Freezes well   Serves 8

2 tablespoons olive or vegetable oil

2 medium onions, chopped

1 green bell pepper, chopped

4 to 5 plump cloves garlic, minced

2 to 3 jalapeño peppers, seeded and minced

$3/4$ teaspoon ground cumin

9 to 10 cups water

1 bay leaf

1 pound black beans, picked over and soaked

$1/4$ to $1/3$ cup dry sherry, optional

Salt to taste, about 1$1/2$ to 2 teaspoons

$1/4$ to $1/2$ teaspoon crushed red chili flakes, optional

Chopped scallions for garnish

Sour cream or nonfat sour cream for garnish

Homemade bacon bits for garnish, optional

1. In a large pot over medium heat, heat the olive oil. Add the onions and bell pepper and sauté, stirring occasionally, until softened, about 7 minutes. Add the garlic, jalapeño, and cumin and cook, stirring occasionally, for 2 minutes.

2. Add the water, bay leaf, and beans. Bring the liquid to a boil. Reduce the heat to medium-low and simmer, partially covered, for 2 to 2$1/2$ hours, or until the beans are tender. Skim off any foam as it forms. Add additional water if too much evaporates.

3. Puree half of the beans in a food processor or blender, or mash in a bowl with potato masher. Alternatively, if you have a hand blender, leave the soup in the pot and partially blend.

4. Return the pureed beans to the pot. Add the sherry and season with salt. Simmer, uncovered, for 10 to 15 minutes.

5. Taste and add the chili flakes, if used. Serve with a dollop of sour cream and garnished with scallions and/or homemade bacon bits.

Garlicky White Bean Soup

This fabulous dish, native to Italy and Southern France, uses home-cooked or canned beans. Serve it with plenty of country-style bread for dunking. The recipe can easily be doubled.

To turn this recipe into a thick puree, as dip for bread or vegetables for hors d'oeuvres or as a side dish, add less, only about $1/3$ to $1/2$ cup broth after pureeing, and stir to make a thick, smooth dip. Drizzle with a small amount extra virgin olive oil before serving.

Garlicky White Bean Soup

Easy   Food Processor, Blender, or Hand Blender
Prep: 15 minutes; Cooking: 30 to 35 minutes   Freezes well   Serves 4 to 6

2 tablespoons olive oil

1 small onion, chopped

1 medium carrot, chopped

1 celery stalk, chopped

3 to 4 plump cloves garlic, minced

$1^{1}/_{2}$ teaspoons minced fresh rosemary, or $3/_{4}$ teaspoon dried

$3^{1}/_{2}$ cups chicken broth or water

3 to $3^{1}/_{2}$ cups cooked white beans, (if using dried, cook $1/_{2}$ pound; if using canned, drain and rinse two 16-ounce cans)

Salt to taste, about $1/_{2}$ to $3/_{4}$ teaspoon

$1/_{4}$ teaspoon freshly ground black pepper

2 tablespoons chopped fresh flat-leaf parsley

1. In a large pot over medium heat, heat the olive oil. Add the onion, carrot, and celery and cook, stirring occasionally, until tender, about 10 minutes. Add the garlic and rosemary and cook, stirring often, for 2 minutes.

2. Add the chicken broth and beans. Cover and simmer for 20 to 25 minutes.

3. Strain the soup, reserving the broth. Puree the beans and vegetables in batches in a food processor or blender with approximately $1^{1}/_{2}$ cups of the broth. Alternatively, if you have a hand blender, leave the soup in the pot and blend.

4. Return the puree, and enough reserved broth to make a good, creamy consistency, to the pot. Reheat over medium heat, stirring occasionally. Season with salt and pepper. Stir in the parsley right before serving.

Chickpea and Sausage Soup

This tasty Mediterranean soup features canned chickpeas and spicy sausage. Use a good quality sausage for the best result.

Chickpea and Sausage Soup

Easy   Prep: 15 minutes; Cooking: 40 minutes
Freezes well   Serves 6

2 tablespoons olive oil

1 medium onion, sliced

1 medium carrot, sliced

1 celery stalk, sliced

2 plump cloves garlic, minced

$1^1/_2$ cups shredded green or savoy cabbage

5 cups chicken broth

One 20-ounce can chickpeas, drained and rinsed

1 medium potato, peeled and diced

$^1/_2$ teaspoon Hungarian sweet paprika

$^1/_2$ teaspoon freshly ground black pepper

$^1/_4$ to $^1/_3$ pound spicy sausage such as chorizo, andouille, or kielbasa, sliced

Salt to taste, about $^1/_4$ to $^1/_2$ teaspoon

1. In a large pot, over medium heat, heat the olive oil. Add the onion, carrot, and celery and sauté, stirring occasionally until softened, about 7 minutes. Add garlic and cabbage and cook, stirring occasionally, for 2 to 3 minutes.

2. Add the chicken broth, chickpeas, potato, paprika, and pepper. Simmer, partially covered, until the potatoes and cabbage are tender, about 25 to 30 minutes.

3. Add the sausage and cook until it is heated through, about 5 minutes. Season with salt.

Souper Bowl Fact

Andouille is a hot Cajun sausage and **chorizo** is a spicy sausage found in Mexico, Portugal, and Southern Africa. **Kielbasa** is a milder but flavorful and garlicky sausage from Poland.

Poor Man's Pinto Bean Soup

This hearty and fragrantly spiced soup features the humble pinto bean and takes advantage of canned beans. It's incredibly easy and delicious and can be made in less than an hour. Pink or red beans can be substituted.

For a spicier version, add $1/2$ to 1 seeded and minced jalapeño along with the garlic in step 1, or add $1/4$ to $1/2$ teaspoon crushed red chili flakes in step 4, just before serving.

Poor Man's Pinto Bean Soup

Easy   Food Processor, Blender, or Hand Blender
Prep: 15 minutes; Cooking: 35 to 45 minutes   Freezes well   Serves 6

2 tablespoons olive oil

1 medium onion, chopped

1 medium carrot, chopped

1 celery stalk, chopped

2 plump cloves garlic, minced

One 14-ounce can plum tomatoes with their juices

$2^1/2$ cups beef, chicken, or vegetable broth

Two 16-ounce cans pinto beans, drained and rinsed, or 3 cups cooked

Three 2-inch by $1/2$-inch strips fresh lemon zest

$1/2$ bay leaf

$1/2$ teaspoon ground allspice or mace

Salt to taste, about $1/4$ to $1/2$ teaspoon

Freshly ground black pepper

2 tablespoons chopped fresh cilantro or parsley

1 to $1^1/2$ teaspoons freshly grated lemon zest

Tabasco on the side, optional

1. In a large pot over medium heat, heat the olive oil. Add the onion, carrot, and celery and sauté, stirring occasionally, until softened, about 10 minutes. Add the garlic and cook, stirring, for 1 minute.

2. Add the tomatoes and break them up into pieces with the back of a wooden spoon. Add the broth, pinto beans, strips of lemon zest, bay leaf, and allspice. Reduce the heat to medium-low. Cover and simmer for 25 to 35 minutes.

3. With a slotted spoon, remove and discard the strips of lemon zest and the bay leaf. Remove half the solids from the pot and pulse in a food processor or blender with a small amount of the liquid until a chunky puree forms. Alternatively, if you have a hand blender, leave the soup in the pot and blend partially.

4. Return the puree to the reserved soup in the pot. Season with salt and pepper. Stir in the cilantro and grated lemon zest. Reheat over medium heat. Serve with Tabasco on the side.

The Least You Need to Know

➤ Put dried beans, split peas, and lentils in a strainer and wash under cold running water, then pick over to remove debris.

➤ Presoak dried beans.

➤ Thin legume soups with additional broth or water if they're too thick.

Chapter 16

Chunky Chowders

In this Chapter

➤ Corn Chowder

➤ Spicy Pumpkin and Corn Chowder

➤ Jalapeño, Tomato, and Corn Chowder

➤ Fresh Salmon Chowder

➤ Fisherman's Chowder

➤ New England Clam Chowder

➤ Manhattan Clam Chowder

Chowders are an all-American soup that is rich, thick, and chunky. Chowder's roots lie in colonial New England's seafaring towns, where it's still standard fare at dockside as well as in city restaurants. The name, however, is a French import—chowder being a derivative of the words *chaudière,* meaning steaming boiler, or *chaudron,* meaning cauldron. Both evoke the image of a piping hot pot of soup.

Chowders were originally made of staples—onions, salt pork, milk or cream, fish or clams, and thickened with cracker-type sea biscuits or bread. Eventually the potato replaced biscuits as thickener in the soup. Now we serve crackers on the side. Tomatoes crept in, creating Manhattan-style versions, much to the dismay of chowder purists. Today, the chowder category also includes hearty corn soups.

Corn Chowder

This filling corn soup can be prepared with yellow or white corn. Although fresh is best, it's still wonderful with frozen corn.

If using fresh corn, add the cobs to the pot when you add the broth so as to impart a more robust corn flavor. Remove and discard the cobs before pureeing.

Corn Chowder

Easy   Food Processor, Blender, or Hand Blender
Prep: 15 minutes; Cooking: 45 to 50 minutes   Freezes well   Serves 6 to 8

4 slices bacon, coarsely chopped

1 medium onion, chopped

$3/4$ teaspoon chopped fresh thyme, or $1/4$ teaspoon dried

2 cups chicken broth

2 cups half-and-half or milk

$3^1/2$ cups fresh or frozen corn kernels

2 medium potatoes, about 12 ounces, peeled and diced

2 tablespoons chopped fresh parsley

Salt to taste, about $1/2$ to $3/4$ teaspoon

Freshly ground black pepper to taste

Tabasco to taste

1. In a large pot over medium heat, cook the bacon. When the bacon is cooked, drain off all but 2 tablespoons of the bacon fat.

2. Add the onion and cook, stirring occasionally, until the onion is lightly golden, about 10 minutes. Add the thyme and stir.

3. Add the broth, half-and-half, corn, potatoes, and parsley. Reduce the heat to medium-low. Cover partially and simmer until the corn and potatoes are tender, about 20 to 25 minutes.

4. Remove half the solids from the pot and pulse in a food processor or blender with a small amount of the liquid until a chunky puree forms. Alternatively, if you have a hand blender, leave the soup in the pot and blend partially.

5. Return the puree to the pot. Season with salt and pepper and reheat. Serve with Tabasco sauce on the side.

Spicy Pumpkin and Corn Chowder

This is one terrific soup! I've used creative license, continuing the chowder (r)evolution, by adding pumpkin puree, another American staple, to corn chowder.

Cayenne intensifies the longer the soup is stored, so if you prepare it ahead or plan to freeze it, use a smaller amount of cayenne than called for, about 1/8 to 1/4 teaspoon.

Spicy Pumpkin and Corn Chowder

*Easy   Food Processor or Blender   Prep: 10 to 15 minutes; Cooking: 35 to 45 minutes
Freezes well   Serves 6 to 8*

1 tablespoon butter or margarine

6 scallions, white part only, sliced; reserve chopped greens for garnish

2 plump cloves garlic, minced

1 tablespoon minced fresh ginger, about 1-inch piece

2 cups chicken broth

2 cups canned pureed pumpkin or pureed cooked butternut

1/4 to 1/2 teaspoon cayenne, or to taste

2 cups frozen corn kernels

1/2 cup cream, half-and-half, or milk

Finely grated zest of 1 small to medium lemon

Salt to taste, about 1/2 to 1 teaspoon

Homemade bacon bits, optional

1. In a large pot over medium-low heat, melt the butter. Add the scallions and sauté, stirring occasionally, until tender, about 5 to 7 minutes. Add the garlic and ginger and cook, stirring, for 1 minute.

2. Add the chicken broth, pumpkin, and cayenne. Increase the heat to medium. Simmer, partially covered, for 15 to 20 minutes.

3. Meanwhile, cook the corn kernels according to package directions. Drain off any liquid. Place the corn in a food processor or blender and add the cream. Pulse until a thick puree forms.

4. Add the corn puree to the pumpkin soup. Add the lemon zest and salt, and stir to blend. Heat thoroughly over medium heat for about 5 to 10 minutes. Garnish with the reserved scallion greens and bacon bits.

To make **butternut puree:** Peel a 2-pound butternut squash. Cut in half, remove the seeds, and cube. Steam, boil, or microwave the butternut until tender. Puree in a food processor or blender until smooth, along with a very small amount of broth, if necessary. Makes approximately 2 cups of puree.

Jalapeño, Tomato, and Corn Chowder

This tangy soup is a wonderful alternative to the traditional milk-based corn chowder. It's lower in fat and calories, but has plenty of flavor.

Replace the potato with a medium sweet potato, peeled and diced, for a colorful variation.

Jalapeño, Tomato, and Corn Chowder

Easy   Food Processor or Blender   Prep: 10 to 15 minutes; Cooking: 1 to 1¼ hours
Freezes well   Serves 6 to 8

2 cups cooked fresh or thawed frozen corn kernels

¹/₃ cup milk or half-and-half

1¹/₂ tablespoons olive oil

1 medium onion, chopped

1 small green bell pepper, chopped

¹/₂ to 1 jalapeño, seeded and minced

2 plump cloves garlic, minced

1 tablespoon tomato paste

³/₄ teaspoon ground cumin

3 cups chicken or vegetable broth

One 14-ounce can chopped tomatoes with their juices

1 medium potato, about 6 to 8 ounces, peeled and diced

Salt to taste, about ¹/₂ to ³/₄ teaspoon

¹/₈ teaspoon cayenne, optional

3 tablespoons chopped fresh cilantro

1. In a food processor or blender, puree 1¹/₂ cups corn kernels with the milk and set aside.

2. In a large pot over medium heat, heat the olive oil. Add the onion and bell pepper and sauté, stirring occasionally, until the onion is translucent, about 5 minutes. Add the jalapeño and garlic and cook, stirring constantly, for 1 to 2 minutes. Add the tomato paste and cook, stirring constantly, about 1 minute. Add the cumin and stir.

3. Add the chicken broth, tomatoes, reserved pureed corn, the remaining 1 cup whole corn kernels, and potato. Cover and simmer for 40 to 45 minutes.

4. Add the salt, cayenne, and cilantro and serve.

Fresh Salmon Chowder

This luxurious soup has become a standard in the Pacific Northwest, where fresh salmon is abundant.

Fresh Salmon Chowder

Easy   Prep: 10 to 15 minutes; Cooking: 50 to 60 minutes
Do not Freeze   Serves 4 to 6

2 tablespoons butter or margarine

3 medium leeks, white part only, sliced

1 medium onion, chopped

1 tablespoon tomato paste

$^1/_2$ cup dry white wine or vermouth

$2^1/_2$ cups homemade fish, vegetable, or chicken broth

2 cups half-and-half or light cream

1 large potato, about 6 to 8 ounces, peeled and diced

1 bay leaf

1 teaspoon paprika

12 to 14 ounces fresh, boneless, skinless salmon filet cut into 1-inch chunks

Salt to taste, about $^1/_2$ teaspoon

$^1/_2$ teaspoon freshly ground black pepper

1 tablespoon chopped fresh parsley, chives, or dill

1. In a large pot over medium heat, melt the butter. Add the leeks and onion and sauté until very tender, about 10 minutes.

2. Add the tomato paste and cook, stirring, for 1 minute. Add the wine and cook, stirring, for 2 minutes. Add the broth, half-and-half, potato, bay leaf, and paprika. Simmer, partially covered, until the potatoes are tender, about 25 to 30 minutes.

3. Reduce the heat to medium-low. Add the salmon and simmer until it is cooked through, about 5 to 7 minutes.

4. Remove the bay leaf. Season with salt, pepper, and herbs and serve immediately, garnished with additional parsley, chives, or dill, if desired.

Souper Bowl Fact

The quality of a fish soup depends on the quality of the fish broth used. Try to make your own—it only takes about 30 minutes. Good chicken broth or vegetable broth is preferable to a poor fish broth.

Fisherman's Chowder

Use whatever firm fish is available fresh in your market. Serve with plenty of crackers—perhaps the traditional oyster crackers—on the side.

Do not use soft-textured fish such as flounder, sole, sea bass, redfish, or trout as they tend to fall apart. Any firmer textured fish will work well.

Fisherman's Chowder

Easy   Prep: 10 to 15 minutes; Cooking: 45 to 55 minutes
Do not freeze   Serves 6

3 tablespoons butter or margarine

1 medium onion, chopped

1 celery stalk, chopped

1 medium carrot, finely diced

2 plump cloves garlic, minced

3 cups homemade fish or chicken broth

2 medium potatoes, about 12 ounces, peeled and diced

1 bay leaf

$1^1/_2$ teaspoons minced fresh thyme or $^3/_4$ teaspoon dried

$1^1/_2$ to $1^3/_4$ cups half-and-half, cream, or milk

$1^1/_4$ pounds firm boneless, skinless white fish filets such as monkfish, cod, haddock, or catfish, cut in $1^1/_2$-inch cubes

Salt to taste, about $^1/_2$ teaspoon

$^1/_4$ teaspoon freshly ground black pepper

2 tablespoons chopped fresh parsley

1. In a large pot over medium heat, melt the butter. Add the onion, celery, and carrot and sauté, stirring occasionally, until the vegetables are nearly tender, about 10 minutes. Add the garlic and cook, stirring often, about 2 minutes.

2. Add the broth, potatoes, bay leaf, and thyme. Cover and simmer until the potatoes are tender, about 20 to 25 minutes.

3. Add the half-and-half and fish. Simmer, uncovered, until the fish is cooked through, about 5 to 7 minutes.

4. Season with salt and pepper. Stir in the parsley.

New England Clam Chowder

This, the most famous of all chowders, originally comes from the Massachusetts' coast. I've given instructions for both fresh and canned clams, as folks who live inland don't always have access to fresh. Serve with crackers or oyster crackers.

New England Clam Chowder

Easy to Intermediate, if using fresh clams
Prep: 15 minutes, or 25 if using fresh clams; Cooking: 45 to 55 minutes
Do not freeze   Serves 8

2 to 3 strips bacon, diced

1 medium onion, chopped

2 cups milk

1 cup clam or fish broth, or $1/2$ cup clam juice and $1/2$ cup water or reserved canned clam liquid, thinned with water to make one cup

12 ounces potatoes, about 2 medium, peeled and diced

1 bay leaf

$1/2$ teaspoon minced fresh thyme leaves, or $1/4$ teaspoon dried

$1/2$ to 1 cup cream

Two $6^{1}/2$-ounce cans clams, with juice reserved for broth; or 1 to $1^{1}/2$ cups fresh cooked clams removed from their shells, about 3 to 4 dozen

Salt to taste, about $1/2$ teaspoon

$1/2$ teaspoon freshly ground black pepper

2 tablespoons chopped fresh parsley

1. In a large pot over medium-low heat, cook the bacon, stirring occasionally, until the fat is rendered and the bacon is nearly cooked through. Add the onion and sauté, stirring occasionally, until translucent, about 5 to 7 minutes.

2. Add the milk, clam broth, potatoes, bay leaf, and thyme. Cover partially and simmer until the potatoes are tender, about 20 to 25 minutes. Do not allow the liquid to boil.

3. Add the cream and clams and cook, uncovered, until the clams are heated through, about 5 minutes.

4. Remove the bay leaf. Season with salt and pepper. Stir in the parsley.

Reduced Fat New England Clam Chowder: Replace the bacon with $1^{1}/2$ tablespoons vegetable oil and $1/4$ to $1/3$ cup chopped ham or Canadian bacon. To start the soup, heat the vegetable oil, then add the ham or Canadian bacon and onion and sauté until the onion is translucent, about 5 minutes. Continue with the recipe, but substitute milk for the cream.

Manhattan Clam Chowder

It's more than just an island in the Hudson—Manhattan is also the tomato-based chowder that sparks a heated debate between its devotees and New England Chowder lovers. The verdict is in: It's a darn good soup.

Use hard-shell clams or quahogs for the chowder recipes. Try to buy littleneck clams, which are small. If the clams are large, such as cherrystone, chop them coarsely after they're cooked.

Manhattan Clam Chowder

Easy to Intermediate, if using fresh clams
Prep: 15 minutes or 25 minutes, if using fresh clams; Cooking: 40 minutes
Do not freeze   Serves 6 to 8

2 tablespoons olive oil

1 medium onion, chopped

1 celery stalk, diced

$^1/_2$ medium green bell pepper, diced

One 28-ounce can plum tomatoes with their juices, broken up with the back of a spoon

$3^1/_2$ cups clam or fish broth, or fish broth only, or $1^1/_2$ cups clam juice and 2 cups water

2 medium potatoes, peeled and diced

1 teaspoon minced fresh thyme, or $^1/_2$ teaspoon dried

1 teaspoon minced fresh basil, or $^1/_2$ teaspoon dried

$^1/_4$ teaspoon minced fresh oregano, or $^1/_8$ teaspoon dried

1 bay leaf

Two $6^1/_2$-ounce cans clams, with juice reserved for broth, or 1 to $1^1/_2$ cups fresh cooked clams, removed from their shells, about 3 to 4 dozen clams

Salt to taste, about $^1/_2$ to $^3/_4$ teaspoon

$^1/_2$ teaspoon freshly ground black pepper

2 tablespoons minced fresh parsley

1. In a large pot over medium heat, heat the olive oil. Add the onion, celery, and bell pepper and sauté, stirring occasionally, until the vegetables are tender, about 10 minutes.

2. Add the tomatoes, broth, potatoes, thyme, basil, oregano, and bay leaf. Cover partially and simmer until the potatoes are tender, about 20 to 25 minutes.

3. Add the clams and cook until the clams are heated through, about 5 minutes. Remove the bay leaf. Season with salt and pepper and stir in the parsley.

The Least You Need to Know

➤ Chowders originated in New England.

➤ Chowders are thick, chunky, and hearty fare.

➤ Serve crackers with fish or shellfish chowders.

Hearty Poultry and Meat Soups

Fortifying and robust, poultry and meat soups are especially enjoyable when the air gets cooler. They are substantial enough to be considered a main course, requiring only bread or crackers and perhaps a salad on the side. In winter, I like to keep them on hand in the freezer. Most chicken soups can be made in a relatively short time, but the meat soups must simmer for an hour or two so that the meat becomes very tender.

Chicken and Corn Soup

Hale and hearty, this traditional American soup comes from the farm kitchens of the Pennsylvania Dutch.

Hard-boiled eggs do not freeze well, so if you want to make a batch of this soup and freeze any leftovers, add the chopped hard boiled eggs to the individual serving bowls, not to the pot. Then leftovers can be frozen without the eggs.

Chicken and Corn Soup

Easy   Prep: 10 minutes; Cooking: 25 minutes   Do not freeze   Serves 6 to 8

$5^1/_2$ cups chicken broth

$^1/_2$ pound boneless chicken breasts, cut into bite-size pieces, or 1 cup cooked cubed chicken

$1^1/_4$ cups fresh or one 10-ounce package frozen corn kernels

2 ounces fine egg noodles, about $1^1/_4$ cups

Salt to taste, about $^1/_2$ to $^3/_4$ teaspoon

$^1/_4$ teaspoon freshly ground black pepper

1 to 2 hard-boiled eggs, chopped

1 tablespoon chopped fresh parsley

1. In a large pot over medium heat, combine the chicken broth, chicken, and corn. Cover partially and simmer for 15 minutes or until the chicken is cooked through.

2. Add the noodles and cook until the noodles are tender, about 8 to 10 minutes. Season with salt and pepper.

3. Remove from the heat. Add the hard-boiled eggs and parsley.

Country Chicken Noodle Soup

Nothing beats this chunky chicken noodle soup on a cool day.

Country Chicken Noodle Soup

Easy   Prep: 10 minutes; Cooking: 25 to 30 minutes   Freezes well   Serves 6 to 8

2 tablespoons vegetable oil

1 small onion, quartered and thinly sliced

1 small celery stalk, finely diced

1 small carrot, finely diced

5^{1}/$_{2}$ cups chicken broth

4 ounces boneless chicken, diced, or ^{1}/$_{2}$ cup diced cooked chicken

^{1}/$_{2}$ teaspoon minced fresh thyme leaves, or ^{1}/$_{4}$ teaspoon dried

1^{1}/$_{2}$ to 1^{3}/$_{4}$ cups short, broad, egg noodles, about 3^{1}/$_{2}$ ounces

1^{1}/$_{4}$ cups fresh or one 10-ounce package frozen peas or string beans

Salt to taste, about ^{1}/$_{2}$ to ^{3}/$_{4}$ teaspoon

^{1}/$_{4}$ teaspoon freshly ground black pepper

1^{1}/$_{2}$ tablespoons chopped fresh parsley

1. In a large pot over medium heat, heat the vegetable oil. Add the onion, celery, and carrot and sauté, stirring occasionally, until softened, about 10 to 15 minutes.

2. Add the broth, chicken, and thyme. Cover and simmer until the chicken is cooked and the vegetables are very tender, about 15 minutes.

3. Add the noodles and peas. Simmer, uncovered, until the noodles are tender, about 10 to 12 minutes. Season with salt and pepper. Stir in the parsley.

Country Turkey Noodle Soups: Gobble, Gobble! Replace the chicken with turkey, and if you have it, use turkey broth instead of chicken. Substitute fine egg noodles for broad.

Old-Fashioned Chicken or Turkey Rice Soup

This simple soup features the true, from-scratch method of making a chicken soup. Vary it by adding a few cooked or frozen vegetables in the last step.

Using a cut-up, meaty, leftover carcass from a roasted turkey or chicken instead of raw chicken parts will work and is economical, but you may need to reinforce the broth by adding a few raw chicken parts or leftover meat; otherwise, the broth may taste too watery and weak.

The process used in this recipe is the conventional way to start many chicken-based soups. In most of the recipes, however, I call for chicken broth and either raw or cooked chopped or shredded chicken added to the broth, which saves a lot of time for the busy cook. If you have the time or the inclination, you can, of course, choose to begin other soups by following this old-fashioned method as laid out in steps 1 through 5.

Old-Fashioned Chicken or Turkey Rice Soup

Easy   Prep: 10 minutes; Cooking: 1¹/₂ to 2 hours   Freezes well   Serves 6

1¹/₂ tablespoons vegetable oil	¹/₂ bay leaf
1 carrot, chopped	6 to 7 cups water
1 celery stalk, chopped	¹/₂ cup white rice
1 small onion, chopped	Salt to taste, about ³/₄ to 1 teaspoon
2 to 2¹/₂ pounds chicken parts, preferably backs, thighs, legs, and wings	Freshly ground black pepper to taste
	Chopped fresh parsley for garnish

1. In a large pot over medium heat, heat the vegetable oil. Add the carrot, celery, and onion and sauté, stirring occasionally, until the onion is translucent, about 5 minutes.

2. Add the chicken parts and the bay leaf and cover with the water. Use additional water if necessary, making sure the chicken is covered totally with water.

3. Cover partially. Place over medium heat and bring to a gentle boil. Skim off any foam.

4. Reduce the heat to medium-low and simmer, partially covered, until the chicken is tender. This should take about 1¹/₂ to 2 hours. Skim off any foam and fat as it forms. Add additional water if too much has evaporated.

5. Strain the solids from the broth and discard the vegetables and bay leaf. Remove the meat from the bones and reserve, but discard the skin and bone. Shred or cut the meat into bite-size pieces.

6. Return the broth to a gentle boil. Add the rice and the reserved meat and simmer, uncovered, until the rice is tender, about 15 to 20 minutes. Season with salt and pepper and garnish with parsley.

Easy Chicken or Turkey Vegetable Soup

Ever-popular chicken soup has many variations. This is another effortless way to make it.

Give this soup an Italian flair by stirring in a tablespoon or two of fresh chopped basil or basil pesto. Serve it with freshly grated Parmesan or Romano cheese.

Easy Chicken or Turkey Vegetable Soup

Easy   Prep: 15 to 20 minutes; Cooking: 35 to 40 minutes   Freezes well   Serves 6 to 8

Broth:

2 tablespoons vegetable or olive oil

1 medium onion, quartered and thinly sliced

1 medium carrot, diced

1 celery stalk, diced; 1 tablespoon of leaves chopped and reserved

1 plump clove garlic, minced, optional

6 cups chicken broth

Use a total of 2 cups of vegetables from these lists:

Root Veggie Choices:

$1/2$ cup chopped turnip or rutabaga

$1/2$ cup diced, peeled potato

$1/2$ cup diced sweet potato

Veggie Choices:

$1/2$ cup fresh or frozen corn kernels

$1/2$ cup fresh or frozen peas

$1/2$ cup fresh or frozen string beans

$1/2$ cup chopped green or savoy cabbage

$1/2$ cup diced zucchini

$1/2$ cup diced yellow squash

$1/2$ drained, canned tomatoes, chopped or stewed

Other Ingredients:

1 to $1^1/2$ cups cooked cubed or shredded chicken or turkey

Salt to taste, about $1/2$ to $3/4$ teaspoon

Freshly ground black pepper to taste

2 tablespoons minced fresh parsley

1. In a large pot over medium heat, heat the vegetable oil. Add the onion, carrot, and celery and sauté, stirring occasionally, until softened, about 10 minutes. Add the garlic and cook, stirring, for 1 minute.

2. Add the broth and any selections from the Root Veggies list. Cover and bring the liquid to a gentle boil. Once it has boiled, cover partially and simmer until the vegetables are almost tender, about 10 to 15 minutes.

3. Add your choices from the Veggie Choices list. Add additional broth if you want to add more veggies than suggested or if the soup is too chunky for you. Stir in the chicken or turkey and simmer, uncovered, until the vegetables are tender, about 10 to 12 minutes.

4. Season with salt and pepper. Stir in the parsley and reserved celery leaves.

Chicken and Sausage Gumbo

Straight from Cajun country to your table, this gumbo is fantastic. Make sure all the ingredients are prepped and ready before you begin making the roux, which is the only tricky step in preparing this soup.

Never rush a roux! A good roux, a combination of vegetable oil and flour, takes plenty of time and should be cooked slowly over low heat. Remember to heat the chicken broth to a gentle simmer. Do not add cold chicken broth or the roux will turn lumpy.

If there are any dark brown or black specks in the roux, it has burned and must be thrown away. You'll need to start from scratch in a clean pot.

Chicken and Sausage Gumbo

Intermediate to Challenging   Prep: 20 minutes; Cooking: 2 to 2¹/₂ hours
Freezes well   Serves 6 to 8

For the Roux:

¹/₃ cup vegetable oil

¹/₃ cup all-purpose flour

For the Gumbo:

1 medium onion, chopped, about ¹/₂ cup

5 scallions, white part only, sliced, about ¹/₄ cup

1 celery stalk, chopped, about ¹/₂ cup

1 small to medium green bell pepper, chopped, about ¹/₂ cup

6 cups chicken broth, heated

1 pound boneless, skinless chicken breasts or thighs, cut into thin, bite-size strips

¹/₄ to ¹/₃ pound andouille or chorizo sausage, sliced

1 to 1¹/₂ teaspoons cayenne, or to taste

¹/₂ teaspoon ground black pepper

¹/₄ teaspoon ground white pepper

¹/₂ teaspoon minced fresh thyme leaves, or ¹/₄ teaspoon dried

Salt to taste, about ¹/₂ to ³/₄ teaspoon

1 tablespoon gumbo filé, optional

2 tablespoons chopped fresh parsley

1¹/₂ cups cooked rice

Tabasco sauce

1. **To make the roux:** In a heavy Dutch oven or deep skillet (preferably cast iron or enameled cast iron) over low heat, combine the oil and flour. Cook, stirring frequently, pushing the mixture off the bottom and stirring in a circular motion, until the roux becomes a rich golden brown color. Although this process can take 45 minutes to 1 hour, be careful not to burn the roux. It should be brown, but not blackened.

2. **To make the gumbo:** Add the onion, scallions, celery, and bell pepper to the roux and increase the temperature to medium-low. Cook, stirring almost constantly, until the vegetables are softened, about 7 to 10 minutes.

continues

3. Gradually ladle in the warmed chicken broth, stirring after each addition. Bring the mixture to a boil and continue stirring.

4. Add the chicken, sausage, 1 teaspoon of the cayenne, black pepper, white pepper, and thyme. Cover partially (or it will boil over and make a mess) and simmer for 45 to 60 minutes. Skim the surface with a ladle to remove any fat that rises.

5. Taste for salt, and season as necessary. You might want to add additional cayenne. Add the gumbo filé and parsley and stir to blend. Serve in soup bowls over rice with Tabasco sauce on the side.

Souper Bowl Fact

Gumbo filé or **filé powder** is made from ground sassafras leaves and has an earthy flavor. Used in Cajun cooking, it is available in the spice section of supermarkets and specialty markets.

Nana's Beef, Vegetable, and Barley Soup

Warming and wonderful, this winter soup is a freezer favorite in my house.

You can replace the frozen vegetables with fresh if you want. You can also substitute peas for the lima beans or string beans, but only add them at the time you would add the string beans.

Nana's Beef, Vegetable, and Barley Soup

Easy   Prep: 15 to 20 minutes; Cooking: 1^1/$_2$ to 1^3/$_4$ hours   Freezes well   Serves 12 to 14

One 28-ounce can whole plum tomatoes with their juices, broken into pieces with the back of a spoon

8 to 10 cups beef broth or water

1 pound beef chuck, cut into 1-inch cubes

1 medium to large onion, quartered and thinly sliced

2 medium carrots, sliced

2 celery stalks, sliced

One 10-ounce package frozen corn kernels

One 10-ounce package frozen lima beans

1^1/$_2$ cups shredded savoy or green cabbage

^{1}/$_3$ cup pearl barley

1 bay leaf

One 10-ounce package frozen string beans

Salt to taste, about ^{1}/$_2$ to 1 teaspoon

Freshly ground black pepper to taste

1. In a large pot over medium heat, combine the tomatoes, 8 cups of the broth, beef chuck, onion, carrots, celery, corn, lima beans, cabbage, barley, and bay leaf. Cover and bring the liquid to a boil.

2. Reduce the heat to medium-low. Simmer, partially covered, until the meat, barley, and vegetables are tender, about 1^1/$_2$ hours. Using a ladle or skimmer, remove any foam that forms during the cooking time.

3. Add the string beans and stir. Thin, if necessary, with the additional broth or water. Simmer for 15 to 20 minutes. Season with salt and freshly ground black pepper.

Spanky's Beef Soup with Tomatoes and Potatoes

Economical and filling, this tasty beef soup is one of the easiest recipes.

Spanky's Beef Soup with Tomatoes and Potatoes

Easy   Prep: 15 minutes; Cooking: 1¼ to 1½ hours   Freezes well   Serves 8

One 14-ounce can whole tomatoes and their juices, broken into pieces with the back of a wooden spoon

4 cups beef broth or water

1 pound beef chuck, cut into 1-inch cubes

1 medium onion, quartered and thinly sliced

2 medium potatoes, about 12 ounces, peeled and diced

2 celery stalks, sliced

1 carrot, sliced

2 plump cloves garlic, peeled and coarsely chopped

½ bay leaf

1 teaspoon fresh thyme leaves, about 1 sprig or ½ teaspoon dried

Salt to taste

Freshly ground black pepper to taste

2 tablespoons chopped fresh flat-leaf parsley

1. In a large pot over medium heat, combine the tomatoes, broth, chuck, onion, potatoes, celery, carrot, garlic, bay leaf, and thyme.

2. Reduce the heat to medium-low. Simmer, partially covered, until the meat and vegetables are tender, about 1¼ to 1½ hours.

3. Remove the bay leaf. Season with salt and pepper and stir in the parsley.

Souper Bowl Fact

Did you ever wonder why ½ a bay leaf is called for? Too much of it will make a dish taste bitter. There are two types of bay leaves. The Turkish variety has smaller leaves and a milder flavor than the California laurel, which is mainly sold in the United States. If you come across fresh bay leaves, use them sparingly because they're quite pungent.

Herbed Oxtail and Vegetable Soup

Oxtail makes an exquisitely rich and flavorful broth. Although this soup takes time, it's well worth the wait.

Because oxtail soup can be fatty, you might want to make it up to a day ahead of serving it. Cool and refrigerate it according to the instructions on p. 81. You can then easily remove the excess fat that has risen to the surface of the cold soup.

Herbed Oxtail and Vegetable Soup

Easy   Prep: 15 to 20 minutes; Cooking: 3 to 3¹/₂ hours   Freezes well   Serves 8 to 10

2 pounds oxtail, cut into sections between the joints

¹/₂ teaspoon salt

¹/₄ teaspoon freshly ground black pepper

1¹/₂ tablespoons olive oil

1 medium onion, chopped

2 carrots, chopped

2 celery stalks, chopped

2 plump cloves garlic, chopped

5¹/₄ cups water

One 14-ounce can tomatoes with their juice, broken with the back of a wooden spoon, or 2 to 3 medium tomatoes, peeled, seeded, and chopped

³/₄ cup hearty red wine or additional water

1 bay leaf

1 teaspoon fresh thyme leaves, or ¹/₂ teaspoon dried

¹/₂ teaspoon fresh chopped rosemary, or dried and crumbled

2 tablespoons chopped flat-leaf parsley

Additional salt to taste, about ¹/₂ to 1 teaspoon

Additional freshly ground black pepper

1. Season the oxtail with salt and pepper. In a large pot over medium heat, heat the olive oil. Add the oxtail and lightly brown each piece on all sides.

2. Add the onion, carrots, celery, and sauté, stirring occasionally for 3 to 4 minutes. Add the garlic and cook, stirring often, for 1 minute.

3. Add the water, tomatoes, wine, bay leaf, thyme, and rosemary. Cover and bring the liquid to a boil.

4. Reduce the heat to medium-low and simmer, partially covered, until the meat is very tender, about 3 to 3¹/₂ hours. Skim off any foam and ladle off visible surface fat, as necessary. Add 1 to 2 cups additional water as the liquid evaporates.

5. Stir in the parsley and season with salt and freshly ground black pepper.

Souper Bowl Fact

Oxtail is the tail of beef or veal and requires slow cooking to become tender. It is normally sold disjointed, but if not, have the butcher cut it into pieces between the joints.

Scotch Broth

Centuries-old, this renowned Scottish soup is always made with lamb or mutton and barley. You may have to look hard for lamb bones—ask your butcher. If you can't find them, leave them out.

For a more robust flavor, make the broth with part water and part beef or chicken broth.

Scotch Broth

Easy   Prep: 15 minutes; Cooking: 1³/₄ to 2 hours
Freezes well   Serves 10 to 12

1¹/₄ to 1¹/₂ pounds lean lamb from shoulder, trimmed and cut into ³/₄-inch cubes

1 pound lamb bones, optional

8 cups water

¹/₂ cup pearl barley

1 medium onion, chopped

1 celery stalk, finely diced

1 medium carrot, finely diced

Salt to taste, about ¹/₂ to 1 teaspoon

¹/₂ teaspoon freshly ground black pepper

2 tablespoons chopped fresh parsley

1. In a large pot over medium heat, combine the lamb, lamb bones, if using them, and water. Cover and bring to a boil. Reduce the heat to medium-low. Simmer, partially covered, for 45 to 55 minutes, skimming off any foam or fat occasionally. With a slotted spoon, remove the bones.

2. Add the barley, onion, celery, and carrot. Simmer, partially covered, until the barley and vegetables are tender, about 50 to 60 minutes. Add additional broth or water, if necessary.

3. Season with salt and pepper and stir in the parsley.

The Least You Need to Know

➤ Serve these hearty soups as a main course.

➤ Make a batch and freeze it.

➤ To thin soup that's too thick, use additional broth, not water.

Chapter 18

CAUTION:HOT!

The Melting Pot

In This Chapter

- ➤ French Onion Soup
- ➤ Minestrone
- ➤ Snow Pea, Mushroom, and Scallion Soup
- ➤ Spanish Garlic Soup with Cheese Dumplings
- ➤ Matzo Ball Soup
- ➤ Italian Chicken, Greens, and Tortellini Soup
- ➤ African Gingered Chicken Rice Soup
- ➤ Hot and Sour Soup
- ➤ Mulligatawny Soup

- ➤ Thai Coconut Chicken Soup
- ➤ Consommé
- ➤ Curried Mussel Soup
- ➤ Indonesian Shrimp Soup with Noodles
- ➤ Japanese Vegetable and Pork Soup
- ➤ Miso Soup
- ➤ Bread Soup
- ➤ Sicilian Fish Soup
- ➤ Hearty Winter Borscht

Many of the best soups on our tables are the popular classics of other countries. Reflecting America's diverse ethnicity and culinary tastes, this varied collection presents treasured recipes from around the world. Ladle up a classic from France, Italy, Russia, Japan, China, Indonesia, India, or Africa.

French Onion Soup

This soup, topped with toasted bread and cheese, is a superb winter entree. Cook the onions slowly to bring out their natural sweetness and, if possible, use homemade broth.

This soup can be made ahead through step 4, then refrigerated or frozen and reheated. Right before serving, it should be completed by baking the soup with the bread-and-cheese topping. Although some restaurants use Mozzarella cheese, the traditional preparation features Swiss or Parmesan cheese.

French Onion Soup

Intermediate to Challenging
Prep: 15 minutes; Cooking: $1^1/_4$ to $1^1/_2$ hours
Freezes well (without bread and cheese)   Serves 6

2 tablespoons butter

2 tablespoon olive or vegetable oil

$1^1/_2$ pounds onions, about 4 to 5 medium, halved and thinly sliced

$^1/_2$ teaspoon minced fresh thyme leaves, or $^1/_4$ teaspoon dried

$^1/_2$ teaspoon salt

$^1/_4$ teaspoon freshly ground black pepper

1 tablespoon all-purpose flour

$^3/_4$ cup dry white wine or vermouth, optional

$5^1/_2$ cups beef or chicken broth

Additional salt to taste, about $^1/_2$ teaspoon

Freshly ground black pepper to taste

6 to 12 slices lightly toasted French or Italian bread, about $^1/_2$- to $^3/_4$-inch thick

$1^1/_2$ cups grated Gruyère or Swiss cheese, or $^3/_4$ cup freshly grated Parmesan cheese

1. In a large pot over medium heat, heat the butter and olive oil. Add the onions and sauté, stirring occasionally, until the onions are a light gold, about 15 minutes. Reduce the heat to medium-low and continue cooking, stirring occasionally, until the onions are a rich golden color, about 30 minutes. This process cannot be rushed.

2. Add the thyme, salt, and pepper and cook for 2 to 3 minutes more. Sprinkle the onions with the flour and cook, stirring almost constantly, for 1 to 2 minutes.

3. Add the wine and cook, stirring constantly, for 1 to 2 minutes. Add the broth. Cover and simmer for 35 to 40 minutes.

4. Season with additional salt and pepper to taste.

5. Preheat the oven to 400°F. Ladle the hot soup into individual ovenproof soup bowls, or into an ovenproof casserole, so that the soup nearly reaches the top of the container, and place on a foil-lined baking sheet. Float the bread on top of the hot soup and sprinkle the toasted bread evenly with the cheese. Bake until the cheese is melted, about 2 to 4 minutes, and serve immediately.

Minestrone

Minestrone is one of Italy's most famous and beloved dishes. The Italian word for soup is *minestra. Minestrone* literally means "big soup." There are many versions of this hearty entree in which vegetables, beans, and pasta join forces. Always serve with freshly grated Parmesan cheese.

Minestrone

Easy

Prep: 20 minutes; Cooking: 50 to 60 minutes   Freezes well   Serves 6

3 tablespoons olive oil

1 medium onion, chopped

2 medium carrots, chopped

2 medium celery stalks, chopped

2 ounces lean ham, diced

2 plump cloves garlic, minced

7 cups chicken or vegetable broth

$1/4$ small savoy or green cabbage, thinly sliced, about $1^{1}/4$ cups shredded

2 small zucchini or yellow squash, cut in half-moons

One 14-ounce can plum tomatoes with their juices, broken into pieces with the back of a spoon

One 15- to 16-ounce can white beans, or pink or red beans, drained and rinsed

2 tablespoons chopped flat-leaf parsley

1 tablespoon chopped fresh basil, or 1 teaspoon dried

$2/3$ cup small elbow macaroni, small shells, or ditalini

Salt to taste, about $1/2$ to $3/4$ teaspoon

$1/2$ teaspoon freshly ground black pepper

Freshly grated Parmesan cheese for garnish

1. In a large pot over medium-low heat, heat the olive oil. Add the onion, carrot, celery, and ham and sauté, stirring occasionally, until the onions are translucent, about 5 to 7 minutes. Add the garlic and cook, stirring often, for 2 minutes.

2. Add the broth, cabbage, zucchini, tomatoes, beans, parsley, and basil. Increase the heat to medium and bring the liquid to a boil.

3. Reduce the heat to medium-low. Simmer, partially covered, for 30 to 40 minutes.

4. Add the macaroni, and simmer until the pasta is tender, about 10 to 12 minutes.

5. Taste and season with salt and pepper. Serve with Parmesan cheese on the side.

Snow Pea, Mushroom, and Scallion Soup

A wonderfully light soup with an Asian touch, this fragrant dish is scented with ginger and Chinese sesame oil.

For a vegetarian version, substitute vegetable or mushroom broth for the chicken broth. Replace the chicken with 2 ounces cubed, firm tofu, adding it with the mushrooms and snow peas.

Snowpea, Mushroom, and Scallion Soup

Easy   Prep: 10 minutes; Cooking: 20 to 25 minutes
Freezes well   Serves 6 to 8

7 cups homemade, unsalted chicken broth

1 tablespoon fresh lemon or lime juice

2 to 3 tablespoons soy sauce or more, to taste

6 scallions, white and green parts, sliced on an angle, with white and green parts kept separate

1 tablespoon minced ginger, about 1-inch piece

3 to 4 ounces ramen or very thin egg noodles, broken in half

$1/2$ pound, about 1 cup cooked, shredded, or cubed chicken

1 tablespoon vegetable oil

6 medium shiitake (stems removed and discarded), cremini, or white mushrooms, sliced

2 ounces snow peas, trimmed and sliced in half crosswise on an angle

$1^1/2$ teaspoons sesame oil

1. In a large pot over medium heat, combine the broth, lemon juice, soy sauce, white part of the scallions, ginger, ramen, and chicken. Cover and simmer 10 to 15 minutes.

3. Meanwhile, in a small skillet, heat the vegetable oil. Add the mushrooms and cook until tender, about 5 minutes. Set aside.

4. Add the mushrooms and snow peas and simmer until the snow peas are tender-crisp, about 3 minutes. Stir in the reserved scallion greens and sesame oil.

Spanish Garlic Soup with Cheese Dumplings

Garlic soup hails from Spain. Many versions are topped with eggs that are poached in the soup. Although not traditional, I add flavorful Parmesan and cornmeal dumplings that are simmered briefly in the soup. (Yummy! What a great idea.)

Spanish Garlic Soup with Cheese Dumplings

Intermediate   Prep: 20 to 25 minutes; Standing: 25 to 30 minutes; Cooking: 40 to 50 minutes   Freezes well   Serves 6

For the Dumplings:

$1/2$ cup cornmeal

$1/2$ cup freshly grated Parmesan or Romano cheese

$1/4$ teaspoon salt

1 teaspoon finely grated onion

2 teaspoons finely minced parsley

2 tablespoons melted butter

1 large egg, lightly beaten

For the Garlic Soup:

2 tablespoons olive oil

14 to 18 plump cloves garlic, peeled

6 cups chicken broth

Salt to taste, about $1/2$ teaspoon

$1/4$ teaspoon freshly ground black pepper, to taste

1. **To prepare the dumplings:** In a small bowl, combine the cornmeal, cheese, and salt. Add the onion and parsley and stir to mix. With a fork, stir in the butter. Make a well in the center of the dry ingredients. Add the egg and stir with a fork. Knead the dough briefly in the bowl until a smooth dough forms, about 1 to 2 minutes.

2. Let the dough rest for 25 to 30 minutes. Form the dough into a rectangle and score evenly with a knife into 18 pieces. Form the pieces into small balls by rolling them gently in the palm of your hand. Set aside. Cover loosely with a clean kitchen towel or plastic wrap to keep them from drying out.

3. **To prepare the garlic soup:** In a medium pot over medium-low heat, heat the olive oil. Add the garlic and cook, turning the cloves once or twice, until they just begin to turn lightly golden, about 5 to 7 minutes. Add the chicken broth, cover, and simmer for 20 to 25 minutes.

4. Remove the garlic cloves with a skimmer or slotted spoon. Puree the garlic with 2 to 3 tablespoons of the hot broth in a food processor or blender, or mash well with a fork. Return the garlic puree to the broth. Season with salt and pepper.

5. **To cook the dumplings:** Bring the broth to a gentle simmer over medium to medium-low heat. Add the dumplings to the broth. Simmer, uncovered, until they are cooked, about 10 minutes. Do not allow the broth to boil vigorously or the dumplings may fall apart.

Matzo Ball Soup

The homespun favorite, the pride of many Jewish grandmothers, features matzo balls and "Jewish penicillin," —otherwise known as chicken soup.

Matzo Ball Soup

Intermediate
Prep: 30 minutes; Standing: 20 minutes to 2 hours; Cooking: 25 to 35 minutes
Freezes well   Serves 6 to 8

For the matzo balls:

2 eggs

$1/2$ teaspoon salt

$1/8$ teaspoon white pepper

Pinch ginger or cinnamon

3 tablespoons broth or water

1 tablespoon vegetable oil

$2/3$ cup matzo meal

For the soup:

6 cups chicken broth

1 cup cooked shredded chicken, optional

2 tablespoons chopped fresh parsley

1 tablespoon snipped fresh dill

1. **To prepare the matzo balls:** In a medium bowl, beat the eggs well. Add the salt, pepper, and ginger. Add the chicken broth and vegetable oil. Add the matzo meal and stir to blend. Cover and let stand 20 minutes, or cover and refrigerate for up to 2 hours. The dough will thicken. With wet hands, form the dough into 12 balls, using about a tablespoon of dough for each ball.

2. **To cook the matzo balls:** Drop the balls into a large pot of lightly salted, boiling water and cook for 15 to 20 minutes. Remove them with a slotted spoon and set aside until you're ready to add to them to the prepared simmering soup.

3. **To prepare the soup:** In a large pot over medium heat, combine the broth and cooked chicken and simmer until hot. Add the matzo balls and heat thoroughly, about 10 minutes. Stir in the parsley and dill.

Souper Bowl Fact

Matzo balls are traditionally made with **schmaltz,** or chicken fat, but I've lightened the recipe and used vegetable oil. Add 1 tablespoon chopped fresh parsley to the dough to add color to the soup.

Italian Chicken, Greens, and Tortellini Soup

Quick and easy, this simple and tasty soup is a wonderful addition to your repertoire.

One of the filled pastas, **tortellini** is a small and doughnut-shaped. It is available frozen, dried, or fresh in the dairy case of most supermarkets. You might need to alter the cooking time slightly, depending on which type you use.

Italian Chicken, Greens, and Tortellini Soup

Easy   Prep: 10 to 15 minutes; Cooking: 20 to 25 minutes   Freezes well   Serves 6 to 8

2 tablespoons olive oil

5 to 6 scallions, white part only, sliced

1 red bell pepper, sliced in thin strips

3 to 4 shiitake (stems removed and discarded), cremini, or white mushrooms, sliced

1 plump clove garlic, minced

6 cups chicken broth

4 ounces cooked, shredded chicken, about $^2/_3$ cup

2 cups thinly sliced greens, such as spinach or escarole

4 ounces cheese or mushroom tortellini

Salt to taste, about $^1/_2$ to $^3/_4$ teaspoon

$^1/_2$ teaspoon freshly ground black pepper

Freshly grated Parmesan, optional

1. In a large pot over medium heat, heat the olive oil. Add the scallions and bell pepper and sauté, stirring occasionally, about 5 minutes. Add the mushrooms and garlic and cook, stirring often, for 2 to 3 minutes.

2. Add the broth. Cover and bring to a boil. Add the chicken, greens, and tortellini. Cover partially and simmer until the greens and tortellini are tender, about 10 minutes. Season with salt and pepper. Serve with Parmesan cheese on the side.

African Gingered Chicken Rice Soup

Scented with ginger, allspice, cardamom, and bay leaf, this unique soup is an outstanding variation of chicken rice soup.

To bring out the most flavor, the spices need to be sautéed with the onions before they are simmered in the broth. If you want to remove the whole spices—allspice, cardamom, and bay leaf—lift them out with a skimmer or slotted spoon before serving.

African Gingered Chicken Rice Soup

Easy   Prep: 10 to 15 minutes; Cooking: 40 minutes   Freezes well   Serves 6

2 tablespoons vegetable oil

1 medium onion, quartered and thinly sliced

2 tablespoons minced fresh ginger, about 2-inch piece

4 whole allspice berries or cloves

4 whole cardamom pods

1 bay leaf

8 ounces boneless chicken breast, cooked and cut into bite-size cubes or strips, about $1^1/_2$ cups

$5^1/_2$ cups chicken broth

$^1/_2$ cup white rice

2 tablespoons fresh lemon or lime juice

Salt to taste, about $^1/_2$ to $^3/_4$ teaspoon

$^1/_2$ teaspoon freshly ground black pepper

$^1/_3$ cup coarsely chopped fresh cilantro

Fresh ginger, peeled and very thinly sliced in matchstick-size strips for garnish, optional

1. In a large pot over medium heat, heat the oil. Add the onion, ginger, allspice berries, cardamom, and bay leaf and sauté, stirring occasionally, until the onions are tender, about 10 to 12 minutes.

2. Add the chicken and cook, stirring occasionally, until the chicken turns white, about 3 to 5 minutes.

3. Add the chicken broth and bring to a gentle boil. Add the rice. Cover partially and simmer until the rice is tender and the chicken is cooked through, about 20 minutes.

4. Add the lemon juice. Season with salt and pepper and simmer for 5 minutes. Stir in the cilantro. Garnish with additional ginger and serve.

Hot and Sour Soup

This recipe is based on the famous soup native to Szechwan province in southwestern China. Feel free to add extra vinegar or chili oil, according to your taste.

To make slicing fresh meat or poultry easier, put it in the freezer for 10 to 15 minutes, then remove and slice it. The meat will be firm enough to make thin slicing an easy task.

Hot and Sour Soup

Easy to Intermediate
Prep: 30 minutes; Cooking: 20 to 25 minutes   Do not freeze   Serves 6

4 to 6 dried wood or cloud ear mushrooms

3 to 4 dried shiitake mushrooms

2¹/₂ tablespoons cornstarch

3 tablespoons water

3 tablespoons rice wine or white wine vinegar

3 tablespoons soy sauce

1 teaspoon freshly ground black pepper

4 cups chicken broth

¹/₄ cup bamboo shoots, cut in thin, matchstick-size strips

¹/₄ pound boneless pork loin chop or boneless chicken breast, very thinly sliced in matchstick-size strips

1¹/₂ teaspoons minced fresh ginger, about ¹/₂-inch piece

3 ounces firm tofu, cubed

1 large egg, beaten

1 tablespoon sesame oil

2 medium scallions, white and green parts, thinly sliced

Chinese chili oil or Tabasco to taste

1. Soak the dried mushrooms in 1¹/₂ cups boiling water for 20 minutes. Strain the liquid through a sieve lined with a paper coffee filter, and reserve the liquid. Cut the mushrooms into very thin strips.

2. In a small bowl combine the cornstarch and water and set aside.

3. In another small bowl, combine the vinegar, soy sauce, and black pepper and set aside.

4. In a large pot over medium heat, heat the broth and reserved mushroom liquid until simmering. Add the mushrooms, bamboo shoots, pork or chicken, ginger, and vinegar mixture and simmer for 2 to 3 minutes.

5. Stir the cornstarch mixture and add it to the pot. Let the liquid come to a boil, add the tofu, and cook for 2 to 3 minutes.

6. While stirring the soup with a fork, pour in the egg and stir until the egg has firmed into fine threads, 1 to 2 minutes.

7. Remove from the heat immediately. Add the sesame oil and chopped scallions. Season to taste with chili oil or Tabasco. Add a small amount of additional vinegar if you want a more sour flavor. Serve immediately.

Mulligatawny Soup

Mulligatawny is a lightly curried chicken soup that hails from Southern India. Here, grated apples add texture and balance the curry. It's your choice to use coconut milk or cream, but always serve the soup over rice.

Curry powder is a blend of several spices ground into a fine powder. It typically includes cardamom, cinnamon, chilies, cloves, coriander, cumin, fennel seed, ground red pepper, black pepper, and turmeric, although a range of other spices can also be added.

Mulligatawny Soup

Easy   Prep: 15 minutes; Cooking 40 to 45 minutes
Freezes well (leave out coconut milk if freezing and add to thawed soup when reheating)
Serves 6 to 8

2 tablespoons vegetable oil

1 medium onion, chopped

2 cloves plump garlic, minced

1 tablespoon minced ginger, about 1-inch piece

1 to 2 tablespoons good-quality curry powder, preferably Madras

3/4 pound boneless chicken breasts or thighs, cut into bite-size cubes

2 medium, sweet apples, such as Golden Delicious or Cortland, peeled and coarsely grated, about 1 3/4 cups

3 to 4 cups chicken broth

3/4 to 1 cup unsweetened coconut milk, half and-half, or cream, optional

Salt to taste, about 1/2 teaspoon

1 cup cooked rice

1. In a large pot over medium heat, heat the vegetable oil. Add the onion and sauté, stirring occasionally, until translucent, about 5 minutes. Add the garlic, ginger, and curry powder and cook, stirring constantly, for 1 to 2 minutes.

2. Add the chicken and cook, stirring occasionally, until the chicken turns white, about 5 minutes. Add the apples and 3 cups of the broth (or 4 cups if not using the coconut milk or half-and-half).

3. Reduce the heat to medium-low. Cover and simmer until the chicken is cooked and the apples are very tender and partially disintegrated, about 25 to 30 minutes. Add the coconut milk or half-and half and salt and heat thoroughly, about 5 minutes.

4. Put a tablespoon or two of the cooked rice into each bowl and ladle the soup over the rice.

Thai Coconut Chicken Soup

This velvety smooth and delicately flavored soup with its hint of chilies creates the perfect contrast of spicy and sweet. Add an extra chili if you want the authentic burn of Thai food.

Thai Coconut Chicken Soup

Easy   Prep: 10 minutes; Cooking: 20 to 25 minutes   Do not freeze   Serves 6

$2\frac{1}{2}$ cups chicken broth

2 cups unsweetened coconut milk

2 tablespoons Thai fish sauce or soy sauce

2 Thai or kaffir lime leaves, optional

2 tablespoons dried lemon grass or 1 fresh stalk, chopped, or 1 teaspoon grated fresh lemon zest

1 teaspoon fresh minced ginger, about $\frac{1}{4}$-inch piece

2 bird's-eye chili peppers or 1 to 2 jalapeños, seeded and minced

12 ounces boneless chicken breasts

2 tablespoons fresh lime juice

1 teaspoon sugar

$\frac{1}{4}$ cup cilantro leaves, whole or minced

1. In a large pot over medium heat, combine the chicken broth, coconut milk, fish sauce, lime leaves, lemon grass, ginger, and chilies. Bring the liquid to a boil.

2. Reduce the heat to medium-low. Add the chicken and simmer for 10 to 15 minutes or until the chicken is cooked through.

3. Add the lime juice and sugar and simmer for 3 to 5 minutes.

Float the cilantro leaves on top or garnish with chopped cilantro.

Souper Bowl Fact

Cilantro, a leafy herb that resembles flat-leaf parsley, is used in Southeast Asian and Mexican cooking. Also called Chinese parsley or coriander, it is actually the leaf of the coriander plant, the seeds of which are used dried and ground.

Consommé

This French classic, a crystal-clear soup, can be served as starter to a dinner menu. Low in calories, it is a dieter's delight.

When ladling the soup into the sieve, make certain that the bottom of the sieve does not touch the already strained consommé, or it will become cloudy again.

For another traditional presentation, add $1/4$ cup of finely diced vegetables, such as carrots and celery, to the consommé. Heat until vegetables are tender, about 5 minutes.

Consommé

Intermediate to Challenging   45 minutes
Freezes well   Serves 4 to 6

$1^1/_2$ quarts homemade chicken or beef broth

3 egg whites

Salt to taste

1. In a large saucepan over medium-low heat, heat the broth until it is gently bubbling but not boiling.

2. In a medium bowl, beat the egg whites until foamy. Add the egg whites to the broth. Stir occasionally until the broth starts to bubble gently. Do not stir again. The foam from the egg white will rise to the surface. Make a hole in the center of the foam with a spoon. Simmer until the foam becomes firmer on the surface, about 20 to 30 minutes. Remove the pot from the burner.

3. Meanwhile, line a sieve with a lightly moistened piece of cheesecloth or a clean dish towel and put it over a deep bowl or large saucepan.

4. Using a wooden spoon, carefully push the foam from the hole in the center back to the sides of the pot. Ladle the consommé out of the hole in the foam into the sieve, and strain.

5. Reheat the strained, clear consommé and season with salt to taste.

Curried Mussel Soup

Mussels accented with a touch of Indian curry are superb, especially in this chunky soup full of tomatoes and potatoes.

Remove freshly cooked mussels from their shells for this soup. If the mussels are large, as farm-raised or cultivated ones can be, cut them in half. Using fresh mussels is best. Occasionally, fishmongers will sell them already cooked and out of the shell. Sometimes you'll find them frozen or canned.

Curried Mussel Soup

Easy (Intermediate if using fresh mussels)
Prep: 10 to 15 minutes for canned, 45 to 60 minutes for fresh mussels;
Cooking: 40 to 45 minutes   Freezes well   Serves 6

2 tablespoons vegetable oil

1 small onion, thinly sliced

1 medium carrot, finely diced

2 plump cloves garlic, minced

2 to 3 teaspoons good-quality curry powder, preferably Madras

1 cup canned chopped tomatoes, or 2 medium tomatoes, peeled, seeded, and chopped

1 medium potato, finely diced

3 cups fish broth, or 1 cup clam juice and 2 cups water

3 to 3^1/$_2$ dozen cooked fresh mussels, or two 3^1/$_2$-ounce cans, drained, with juice reserved for broth

Salt to taste, about ^{1}/$_2$ to ^{3}/$_4$ teaspoon

Freshly chopped cilantro or parsley for garnish

1. In a large pot over medium heat, heat the vegetable oil. Add the onion and carrot and sauté until the onion is lightly golden, about 10 to 15 minutes. Add the garlic and curry powder and cook, stirring constantly, for 2 minutes.

2. Add the tomatoes and cook, stirring, for 2 minutes. Add the potato and broth. Cover and simmer until the potato is tender, about 20 minutes.

3. Add the mussels and salt and simmer until heated through, about 3 to 5 minutes. Garnish with chopped cilantro.

Indonesian Shrimp Soup with Noodles

Noodle soups are a staple throughout much of Asia, including Indonesia. They can feature chicken, pork, beef, vegetables or, as in this incredibly light version, shrimp.

Indonesian Shrimp Soup with Noodles

Easy   Prep: 20 minutes; Cooking: 20 to 25 minutes   Do not freeze   Serves 4 to 6

3 cups shrimp, fish, or vegetable broth

2 tablespoons fresh lemon juice

1 tablespoon soy sauce

1 tablespoon dark brown sugar

2 plump cloves garlic, minced

1¹/₂ teaspoons minced ginger, about ¹/₂-inch piece

4 ounces ramen-style noodles or thin Chinese egg noodles

¹/₂ pound medium shrimp, peeled and deveined

2 birds-eye chili peppers or jalapeños, seeded and thinly sliced

1 scallion, white and green parts, cut into ¹/₂-inch pieces

¹/₂ medium cucumber, peeled, seeded, and cut into very thin strips, about 1-inch long (about ³/₄ cup)

1 cup fresh mung bean sprouts

1 tablespoon fresh chopped mint or cilantro

1. In a large pot over medium heat combine the broth, lemon juice, soy sauce, sugar, garlic, and ginger. Simmer for 10 to 15 minutes.

2. Add the noodles and cook until tender, about 3 to 5 minutes, or cook according to package directions.

3. Add the shrimp and the chilies to the broth and cook until shrimp turn pink and begin to curl, about 3 minutes. Do not overcook the shrimp.

4. Remove the soup from the heat and add the scallions and cucumber.

5. To serve, ladle the soup into bowls and divide the bean sprouts equally on top. Garnish with chopped mint or cilantro.

Souper Bowl Fact

There's more than one type of bean sprout: alfalfa, used in salads, and mung bean, which are often found in Chinese and Asian dishes. Mung bean sprouts are found either fresh and canned, but the canned ones lack both crispness and flavor. If you can't find fresh for this recipe, omit them.

Japanese Vegetable and Pork Soup

This uncomplicated soup highlighted with ginger is quick to prepare and very good.

Japanese Vegetable and Pork Soup

Easy   Prep: 10 minutes; Cooking: 25 to 35 minutes   Do not freeze   Serves 4 to 6

1$^{1}/_{2}$ tablespoons vegetable oil

$^{1}/_{4}$ pound ground lean pork or chicken

2-inch piece daikon, quartered and cut into very thin strips, or 5 medium radishes, sliced and cut into thin strips

2-inch piece carrot, quartered and cut into very thin strips

4$^{1}/_{2}$ cups dashi (p. 112) or chicken broth

1 to 2 tablespoons soy sauce

3 to 4 shiitake (stems removed and discarded) or white mushrooms, sliced

2 ounces firm tofu, cubed

1 scallion, white and green parts, cut into $^{1}/_{2}$-inch pieces

2 tablespoons grated fresh ginger, about a 1$^{1}/_{2}$- to 2-inch piece

1. In a large pot over medium heat, heat the vegetable oil. Add the pork and cook, stirring occasionally and breaking up any lumps, until the pork is cooked through, about 7 minutes. Add the daikon and carrot and stir-fry for 3 minutes.

2. Add the dashi and season with soy sauce, the amount depending on the saltiness of the broth itself. Simmer for 5 minutes.

3. Add the mushrooms and tofu and cook until the mushrooms are tender, about 3 to 5 minutes. Do not let the soup boil.

4. Add the scallion and remove the soup from the heat.

5. Wrap the grated ginger in a piece of cheesecloth. Hold the cloth over the soup and wring gently to squeeze out the juice into the soup. Serve immediately.

Souper Bowl Fact

Daikon, a long white root with a sweet flavor and crisp texture, is used in Japanese cooking. It is a wonderful addition to soups, salads, and stir–fries.

Miso and Vegetable Soup

Miso, a mainstay of the Japanese diet, is made from fermented soybean paste and is often used in soups. In Japan, some miso soups are eaten for breakfast, but feel free to eat this one for a surprisingly fast lunch or dinner.

Miso and Vegetable Soup

Easy   15 to 20 minutes
Do not freeze   Serves 4 to 6

4 cups dashi (p. 112) or chicken broth

1 teaspoon soy sauce

2 tablespoons sake or rice wine, optional

2-inch piece daikon, quartered and sliced in thin strips

3-inch piece carrot, halved and sliced in thin strips

3 green beans, cut into 1-inch pieces

3 tablespoons light or red miso or a combination of the two

2 ounces firm tofu, cubed, optional

1 scallion, white and green parts, cut into $1/2$-inch pieces

1. In a large pot over medium heat, bring the dashi, soy sauce, and sake to a gentle simmer. Add the daikon, carrot, and green beans and simmer until tender-crisp, about 3 to 5 minutes.

2. In a small bowl, combine the miso with $1/3$ cup of the simmering broth and stir to dissolve the miso completely.

3. Add the miso mixture to the pot gradually, making sure there are no lumps. Add the tofu. Let the soup heat thoroughly, but don't let it boil or the flavor of the miso will be ruined. Add the scallion and serve immediately.

Souper Bowl Fact

There are several types of **miso**—barley miso, rice miso, and soy miso—and it comes in a variety of colors, from light golden to reddish to a rich brown. High in protein and B vitamins, it also has a high sodium content. Refrigerate any unused miso in an airtight container.

Bread Soup

Made with fresh tomatoes and stale bread, versions of this soup are found in Italy, most notably in Tuscany and Calabria-Lucania.

Although it can also be successfully prepared with canned tomatoes, ripe fresh tomatoes are best! It can be served hot or, my preference, at room temperature.

An alternative way of serving this soup is to put the torn bread into each bowl and ladle the soup on top.

Bread Soup

Easy
Prep: 15 to 20 minutes; Cooking: 30 to 35 minutes;
Standing: (if serving at room temperature) 45 to 60 minutes   Do not freeze   Serves 6

3 tablespoons extra virgin olive oil

1 small onion, chopped

1 celery stalk, chopped

2 to 3 plump cloves garlic, minced

$^1/_4$ teaspoon crushed red chili flakes or $^1/_2$ jalapeño, seeded and minced

$1^1/_2$ pounds ripe tomatoes, peeled, seeded, and coarsely chopped or one 28-ounce can Italian plum tomatoes, drained and coarsely chopped or broken up with the back of a wooden spoon

$2^1/_2$ cups chicken or vegetable broth

$^1/_2$ bay leaf

Salt to taste, about $^1/_2$ to 1 teaspoon

$^1/_4$ teaspoon freshly ground black pepper

4 to 6 slices stale Italian bread, or fresh Italian bread, lightly toasted

$1^1/_2$ tablespoons chopped fresh basil

Freshly grated Romano or Parmesan cheese

1. In a large pot over medium heat, heat the olive oil. Add the onion and celery and sauté, stirring occasionally, until almost tender, about 10 minutes. Add the garlic and chili flakes and cook, stirring constantly, for 1 minute.

2. Add the tomatoes and cook, stirring occasionally, for 7 to 10 minutes.

3. Add the broth and bay leaf and simmer for 10 to 15 minutes. Season with salt to taste and black pepper.

4. Tear the bread into small pieces and add to the soup. Let stand for 2 to 3 minutes. Stir in the basil. Serve with Romano cheese on the side. Serve hot or at room temperature. If serving at room temperature, let stand until cooled, about 45 to 60 minutes.

Sicilian Fish Soup

Like many Mediterranean fish soups, this one uses a combination of seafood: white fish fillets and scallops. The broth is enhanced with herbs, orange zest, and chili flakes.

Add a few cleaned clams or mussels when you add the fish. Discard any that have not opened.

Sicilian Fish Soup

Easy   Prep: 10 to 15 minutes; Cooking: 30 to 35 minutes
Do not freeze   Serves 4 to 6

2 tablespoons olive oil

1 medium onion, chopped

1 celery stalk, chopped

2 to 3 plump cloves garlic, chopped

3$^{1}/_{2}$ cups fish or vegetable broth, or 1$^{1}/_{2}$ cups clam juice and 2 cups water

$^{1}/_{2}$ cup dry white wine or vermouth

1$^{1}/_{2}$ cups chopped canned tomatoes or peeled and seeded fresh tomatoes, about 3 medium

2-inch strip orange or lemon zest

1 teaspoon minced fresh thyme leaves, or $^{1}/_{2}$ teaspoon dried

$^{1}/_{2}$ bay leaf

$^{1}/_{4}$ teaspoon red chili flakes, optional

1 pound combination of fish fillets such as cod, grouper, tilefish, scrod, monkfish, snapper, or other firm-textured white fish, cut into 1$^{1}/_{2}$-inch strips or chunks

$^{1}/_{2}$ pound sea scallops (or an additional $^{1}/_{2}$ pound of fish)

3 tablespoons chopped fresh flat-leaf parsley

3 to 4 slices Italian bread, lightly toasted

1. In a large pot over medium heat, heat the olive oil. Add the onion and celery and cook, stirring occasionally, about 5 to 7 minutes. Add the garlic and cook, stirring often, for 1 minute.

2. Add the fish broth, wine, tomatoes, orange zest, thyme, bay leaf, and chili flakes. Cover and simmer for 15 minutes.

3. Add the fish and scallops and simmer, uncovered, until the fish is cooked through, about 10 minutes.

4. Stir in the parsley. To serve, tear the bread in pieces and put into soup bowls. Ladle the soup on top.

Hearty Winter Borscht

Borscht is a soup from Russia, the Ukraine, and Poland with many variations. Some are hot, some cold, but they all contain beets. This robust version combines beets, cabbage, and beef and should always be served hot.

Hearty Winter Borscht

Easy   Prep: 15 minutes; Cooking: 1¹/₄ to 1¹/₂ hours
Freezes well   Serves 6 to 8

1 pound beef chuck, cut into ¹/₂-inch cubes

6 cups beef broth or water

³/₄ pound beets

1 medium onion, thinly sliced

1 medium carrot, finely diced

1¹/₂ cups shredded cabbage

One 14-ounce can chopped tomatoes, drained

1 bay leaf

2 tablespoons white wine vinegar or fresh lemon juice

2 teaspoons sugar

Salt to taste, about ¹/₂ teaspoon

¹/₂ teaspoon freshly ground black pepper

Sour cream for garnish

Snipped fresh dill for garnish, optional

1. In a large pot over medium heat, combine the beef and water and simmer, partially covered, until the meat is almost tender, about 35 to 40 minutes.

2. Meanwhile, put the beets in a medium saucepan and cover with plenty of cold water. Boil the beets until tender and drain in a colander. When the beets are cool enough to handle, peel and cut them into bite-size wedges and set aside.

3. Add the onion, carrot, cabbage, tomatoes, and bay leaf to the meat. Simmer, covered, until the vegetables and meat are tender, about 30 to 35 minutes longer.

4. Add the beets, vinegar, and sugar and simmer, partially covered, for 15 to 20 minutes. Serve garnished with a dollop of sour cream and dill.

Souper Bowl Fact

The word **vinegar** is derived from the French *vin aigre,* which literally means sour wine. Some vinegars, particularly distilled white vinegar, are very acidic and bitter. Wine vinegars, however, have a pleasingly tart aroma and taste.

The Least You Need to Know

➤ Ethnic soups offer a culinary tour.

➤ Most countries have delicious specialties. Some are filling enough to be a main dish, others are light enough to be served as starters.

➤ When planning a meal, keep the entire menu ethnic.

Cream Soups and Bisques

In This Chapter

Cream soups and bisques are the delightfully rich-tasting, velvety-textured soups that are no longer off-limits to those worried about fat content. Lightened in response to modern dietary concerns, most of these soups are thickened with vegetable purees rather the traditional roux of butter and flour, and they are enriched with a minimum of milk, half-and-half, or cream. Two-percent milk is acceptable, but skim would make the soup too watery. Use whichever you prefer.

In most cases, if you divide the amount of cream or milk in the recipe by the number of portions, you'll find that each serving has only a tablespoon or two. If you prefer, omit the milk or cream and thin the soup with whatever broth or juice is used in the recipe, but keep in mind that dairy products are an excellent source of calcium.

Creamy Potato Leek Soup

Famous from France to Ireland, this filling soup, made of pureed potatoes and leeks, is a heavenly combination.

For a colorful variation, make this soup with 1 pound of potatoes and $1/2$ pound of carrots or parsnips, peeled and thinly sliced.

Creamy Potato Leek Soup

Easy   Food Processor, Blender, or Hand Blender
Prep: 15 minutes; Cooking: 45 minutes   Freezes well   Serves 6

2 tablespoons butter

3 medium leeks, white part only, thinly sliced

1 medium onion, thinly sliced

4 cups chicken broth

$1^1/2$ pounds potatoes, about 3 to 4 medium, peeled and thinly sliced

$1/2$ to $3/4$ cup cream, half-and-half, or milk

Salt to taste, about $1/2$ teaspoon

$1/4$ teaspoon black pepper

Chopped parsley for garnish

1. In a large pot over medium-low heat, melt the butter. Add the leeks and onions and sauté, stirring occasionally, until very tender and lightly golden, about 10 to 15 minutes.

2. Add the broth and potatoes. Increase the heat to medium and bring the liquid to a boil. Simmer, partially covered, until potatoes are tender, about 25 to 30 minutes.

3. Puree in batches in a food processor or blender until smooth. Alternatively, if you have a hand blender, leave the soup in the pot and blend.

4. Return the soup to the pot. Thin with the cream. Add salt to taste and pepper. Heat thoroughly over medium heat. Serve garnished with chopped parsley.

Cream of Carrot Soup with Nutmeg

This inexpensive soup has a glorious orange color and spectacular taste.

Cream of Carrot Soup with Nutmeg

Easy   Food Processor, Blender, or Hand Blender
Prep: 10 to 15 minutes; Cooking: 35 to 45 minutes   Freezes well   Serves 6 to 8

1¹/₂ tablespoons butter or margarine

1 medium onion, chopped

4 cups chicken broth

1¹/₂ pounds carrots, peeled and coarsely chopped

¹/₂ bay leaf

³/₄ to 1 cup cream, half-and-half, or milk

¹/₄ teaspoon freshly ground nutmeg

Salt to taste, about ¹/₂ teaspoon

¹/₈ teaspoon white pepper

1¹/₂ tablespoons snipped fresh dill or chopped chives

1. In a large pot over medium heat, melt the butter. Add the onion and sauté, stirring occasionally, until translucent, about 5 minutes.

2. Add the chicken broth, carrots, and bay leaf. Bring the liquid to a boil. Reduce the heat to medium-low. Cover and simmer until the carrots are tender, about 35 to 40 minutes.

3. Remove the bay leaf. Strain, reserving the broth. Puree the vegetables with some broth in batches in a food processor or blender. Alternatively, if you have a hand blender, leave the soup in the pot and blend.

4. In the same pot, combine the pureed vegetables, reserved broth, and half-and-half. Season with nutmeg, salt, and pepper. Reheat over medium heat, then stir in the dill.

Souper Bowl Fact

Carrots, a member of the parsley family, are an excellent source of the antioxidant beta-carotene, which the body turns into vitamin A. Beta-carotene is also found in broccoli, sweet potatoes, and spinach.

Cream of Carrot Orange Soup

Fresh orange juice and zest add spark to the carrots in this simple soup.

For a change, use fresh tangerine juice and zest instead of orange.

Cream of Carrot Orange Soup

Easy   Food Processor, Blender, or Hand Blender
Prep: 10 to 15 minutes; Cooking: 35 to 45 minutes   Freezes well   Serves 6 to 8

$1^1/_2$ tablespoons butter or margarine

1 medium onion, chopped

$2^1/_2$ cups chicken broth

$1^1/_2$ cups fresh orange juice

$1^1/_2$ pounds carrots, peeled and coarsely chopped

$1/_2$ bay leaf

$3/_4$ to 1 cup cream, half-and-half, or milk

$1^1/_2$ teaspoons freshly grated orange zest

$1/_4$ teaspoon freshly ground nutmeg

Salt to taste, about $1/_2$ teaspoon

$1/_8$ to $1/_4$ teaspoon cayenne

$1/_8$ teaspoon white pepper

$1^1/_2$ teaspoons chopped fresh basil or chervil for garnish

$1^1/_2$ teaspoons chopped fresh chives or fresh chervil sprigs for garnish

1. In a large pot over medium heat, melt the butter. Add the onion and sauté, stirring occasionally, until translucent, about 5 minutes.

2. Add the chicken broth, orange juice, carrots, and bay leaf. Bring the liquid to a boil. Reduce the heat to medium-low. Cover and simmer until the carrots are tender, about 35 to 40 minutes.

3. Remove the bay leaf. Strain, reserving the broth. Puree the vegetables with some broth in batches in a food processor or blender. Alternatively, if you have a hand blender, leave the soup in the pot and blend.

4. In the same pot, combine the pureed vegetables, reserved broth, and half-and-half. Season with orange zest, nutmeg, salt, pepper, and cayenne. Reheat over medium heat. Garnish with the herbs before serving.

Cream of Mushroom Soup

Not at all like its gloppy canned counterpart, this mushroom soup is light, with plenty of mushroom flavor.

Use a combination of white, cremini, and shiitake (no stems) mushrooms for an earthier, richer taste.

Cream of Mushroom Soup

Easy   Prep: 10 to 15 minutes; Cooking: 20 to 25 minutes
Freezes well   Serves 4 to 6

2 tablespoons olive oil

2 tablespoons butter or margarine

1 medium onion, chopped

$1/2$ pound white or cremini mushrooms, coarsely chopped

3 tablespoons all-purpose flour

$2^1/2$ cups mushroom, chicken, or beef broth

2 tablespoons dry sherry, optional

$1/3$ to $1/2$ cup half-and-half, cream, or milk

Salt to taste, about $1/2$ teaspoon

Freshly ground black pepper to taste

1 tablespoon chopped fresh chives or parsley, optional

1. In a medium saucepan over medium heat, heat the olive oil and butter. Add the onion and sauté, stirring occasionally, until translucent, about 5 minutes. Add the mushrooms and cook, stirring occasionally, for 5 minutes more.

2. Add the flour and cook, stirring often, for 2 to 3 minutes.

3. Gradually pour in the broth, stirring after each addition. The soup should begin to thicken. Add the sherry.

4. Bring the soup to a boil, cover and simmer for 5 to 10 minutes. Add the cream and heat through. Season with salt and pepper. Stir in the chives.

Souper Bowl Fact

Sometimes a food processor doesn't get a soup as finely textured as you'd like. For a smoother and lighter soup, after conbining the puree and broth, strain the soup by placing a sieve over a bowl. Pour the soup through, pushing the puree through with the back of a wooden spoon. Discard any remains of the puree from the strainer. Return to the pot, add cream or other liquid if the recipe calls for it, reheat, and serve. This technique can also be used for other soups when you'd like an especially creamy, velvety texture.

Tomato Orange Bisque

This unusual tomato soup is based on an old recipe from the Western Cape Province of South Africa. It's a knockout.

This soup is delightful cold, especially on a sweltering summer day. Chill the cooled soup in the refrigerator for 1 to 1^1/$_2$ hours.

Tomato Orange Bisque

Easy   Food Processor, Blender, or Hand Blender
Prep: 15 minutes; Cooking: 50 to 60 minutes   Freezes well   Serves 4 to 6

2 tablespoons olive oil

1 medium onion, chopped

1 carrot, chopped

1^1/$_2$ cups chicken broth

One 28-ounce can plum tomatoes with their juices

^{1}/$_2$ cup fresh orange juice

1 bay leaf

^{1}/$_2$ teaspoon minced fresh thyme, or ^{1}/$_4$ teaspoon dried

1^1/$_2$ cups cream, half-and-half, or milk

2 teaspoons finely grated fresh orange zest

Salt to taste, about ^{1}/$_2$ to ^{3}/$_4$ teaspoon

1. In a medium pot over medium heat, heat the olive oil. Add the onion and carrot and sauté, stirring occasionally, until translucent, about 5 minutes.

2. Add the broth, tomatoes, orange juice, bay leaf, and thyme. Simmer, partially covered, for 40 to 45 minutes.

3. With a slotted spoon, remove the bay leaf. Puree in batches in a food processor or blender until smooth. Alternatively, if you have a hand blender, leave the soup in the pot and blend.

4. Return the soup to the pot. Add the cream, orange zest, and salt and stir to blend. Reheat over medium heat, stirring occasionally.

Cream of Tomato Soup Variations

I always think of this soup as comfort food. Here are two healthful ways to prepare it.

Cream of Tomato Soup Variations

Easy   Food Processor, Blender, or Hand Blender
Prep: 15 minutes; Cooking: 50 to 60 minutes   Freezes well   Serves 4 to 6

Version 1: Prepare *Creamy Tomato Orange Bisque* on p. 190. Substitute an additional $1/2$ cup chicken broth for the orange juice. Add 2 to 4 teaspoons sugar when adding the tomatoes and broth. Omit the grated fresh orange zest. Garnish with homemade croutons.

Version 2: Prepare *Tomato Basil Soup* on p. 121. After pureeing the ingredients, add $1/2$ to $2/3$ cup cream, half-and-half, or milk and reheat. Omit the basil or pesto if you want.

Souper Bowl Fact

Andy Warhol created his renowned, pop-art lithograph of a Campbell's Tomato Soup can in 1965.

Easy Creamy Spinach Soup

This lovely soup, thickened with rice, is a snap to make and always delicious.

This is a good soup to make when unexpected guests stay for lunch or supper, because you're likely to have the ingredients on hand.

Easy Creamy Spinach Soup

Easy   Food Processor, Blender, or Hand Blender
Prep: 5 to 10 minutes; Cooking: 30 to 35 minutes   Freezes well   Serves 6

2 tablespoons vegetable oil

1 medium onion, chopped

3^1/$_2$ cups chicken broth

^{1}/$_4$ cup white rice

One 10-ounce package frozen, chopped spinach

^{1}/$_2$ teaspoon freshly ground black pepper

^{1}/$_8$ teaspoon ground nutmeg

Salt to taste, about ^{1}/$_2$ teaspoon

^{1}/$_2$ to ^{3}/$_4$ cup half-and-half, cream, or milk

1. In a large pot over medium heat, heat the vegetable oil. Add the onion and sauté, stirring occasionally, until translucent, about 5 minutes.

2. Add the chicken broth and rice. Cover and bring the liquid to a boil. Reduce the heat to medium-low and simmer, partially covered, until the rice is tender, about 15 to 20 minutes.

3. Add the spinach, pepper, and nutmeg. Simmer until the spinach is cooked, about 10 minutes.

4. Puree in batches in a food processor or blender until smooth. Alternatively, if you have a hand blender, leave the soup in the pot and blend.

5. Return the soup to the pot and season with salt. Reduce the heat to medium-low, add the cream, and heat thoroughly.

Cream of Asparagus Soup

This delicate soup is a real spring treat and should be made with fresh asparagus, which is available from February through June. When it is out of season, imports are available, but they can be costly.

Instead of using the whole spear, reserve the tender tips for a side dish and make the soup with only the 1 pound of trimmed stalks.

Cream of Asparagus Soup

Easy   Food Processor, Blender, or Hand Blender
Prep: 10 minutes; Cooking: 20 to 25 minutes   Freezes well   Serves 4 to 6

1 pound asparagus, washed and trimmed

2 tablespoons butter or margarine

1 medium onion, chopped

$1/3$ cup dry white wine or vermouth, optional

3 cups chicken stock

1 cup cream or half-and-half

Salt to taste, about $1/2$ teaspoon

$1/8$ teaspoon white pepper

Freshly grated Romano cheese for garnish, optional

1. Slice off the asparagus tips at an angle and reserve, about 1 cup. Coarsely chop the stalks. Set aside.

2. In a large pot over medium heat, melt the butter. Add the onion and sauté, stirring occasionally, until tender, about 10 minutes. Add the white wine and cook for 1 to 2 minutes.

3. Add the chicken broth. Cover and bring the broth to a boil. Add the chopped stalks and cook, covered, until the stalks are very tender, about 10 to 12 minutes.

4. Puree in batches in a food processor or blender until smooth. Alternatively, if you have a hand blender, leave the soup in the pot and blend.

5. Return the soup to the pot over medium heat. Add the cream and reserved asparagus tips. Season with salt and pepper and simmer until the tips are tender-crisp. Serve with freshly grated Romano cheese on the side.

Cream of Cauliflower Soup

Being a cauliflower lover, I think this is the ultimate cream soup. It's marvelous with the cream or milk, or even without it if thinned with additional broth.

Cream of Cauliflower Soup

Easy   Food Processor, Blender, or Hand Blender
Prep: 10 minutes; Cooking: 40 to 45 minutes   Freezes well   Serves 6 to 8

2 tablespoons butter or margarine

1 small onion, chopped

$1/2$ cup dry white wine or vermouth, optional

$4^1/2$ cups chicken or vegetable broth

$1^1/4$ pounds cauliflower, coarsely chopped, about 6 cups

1 cup cream, half-and-half, or milk

Salt to taste, about $1/2$ to $3/4$ teaspoon

$1/8$ teaspoon white pepper

1. In a large pot over medium heat, melt the butter. Add the onion and cook, stirring occasionally, until translucent, about 5 minutes.

2. Add the wine and cook for 2 minutes. Add the broth and cauliflower. Cover and simmer until the cauliflower is very tender, about 30 to 35 minutes.

3. Puree in batches in a food processor or blender until smooth. Alternatively, if you have a hand blender, leave the soup in the pot and blend.

4. Return the soup to the pot and add the cream. Season with salt and pepper and reheat over medium heat.

Souper Bowl Fact

Broccoflower, the offspring of the cauliflower and broccoli, has a milder flavor and would be suitable for any of the soups that feature either of its parents.

Cream of Broccoli Soup

If you're a broccoli fan, this easy soup will hit the spot.

If you want, you can prepare the soup with chopped stems only (about 6 cups), and reserve the florets for another use.

Cream of Broccoli Soup

Easy   Food Processor, Blender, or Hand Blender
Prep: 10 minutes; Cooking: 45 to 50 minutes   Freezes well   Serves 6 to 8

2 tablespoons butter or margarine

1 small onion, chopped

5 cups chicken or vegetable broth

1 1/4 pounds broccoli, coarsely chopped, about 6 cups

1 cup cream, half-and-half, or milk

Salt to taste, about 1/2 to 3/4 teaspoon

1/4 teaspoon freshly ground black pepper

1. In a large pot over medium heat, melt the butter. Add the onion and cook, stirring occasionally, until translucent, about 5 minutes.

2. Add the broth and broccoli. Cover and simmer until the broccoli is very tender, about 30 to 35 minutes.

3. Puree in batches in a food processor or blender until smooth. Alternatively, if you have a hand blender, leave the soup in the pot and blend.

4. Return the soup to the pot and add the cream. Season with salt and pepper and reheat over medium heat.

Souper Bowl Fact

A nutritional superstar, broccoli is an excellent source of vitamins A and C as well as calcium, iron, and fiber.

Broccoli Cheddar Soup

Not much can top the super duo of broccoli and cheese. This soup has a luxuriously rich texture and taste.

Use medium, sharp, or extra-sharp cheddar, whichever you prefer, in the soups.

Broccoli Cheddar Soup

Easy   Food Processor, Blender, or Hand Blender
Prep: 10 minutes; Cooking: 45 to 50 minutes   Do not freeze   Serves 6 to 8

2 tablespoons butter or margarine

1 medium onion, chopped

4 cups chicken or vegetable broth

1 pound broccoli, coarsely chopped, about 4 to 5 cups

$^1/_2$ cup cream, half-and-half, or milk

6 ounces grated cheddar cheese

Salt to taste, about $^1/_4$ to $^1/_2$ teaspoon

Freshly ground black pepper to taste

1. In a large pot over medium heat, melt the butter. Add the onion and sauté, stirring occasionally, until translucent, about 5 minutes.

2. Add the broth and broccoli. Cover and simmer until the broccoli is very tender, about 35 to 40 minutes.

3. Puree in batches in a food processor or blender until smooth. Alternatively, if you have a hand blender, leave the soup in the pot and blend.

4. Return the soup to the pot over medium heat, add the cream and cheese, and stir until the cheese is melted. Season with salt and pepper.

Souper Bowl Fact

White cheddar is uncolored; yellow is colored with annatto, a natural dye.

Creamy Cheddar Cheese Soup

Red bell pepper and cheddar cheese give this soup, thickened with potatoes, an outstanding taste. It's too filling to be served as anything other than the main course. If you like it hotter, add extra cayenne or serve with Tabasco on the side.

To peel the bell pepper easily, slice off the top and bottom ends and cut the pepper in half. Peel with a vegetable peeler.

Creamy Cheddar Cheese Soup

Easy   Food Processor, Blender, or Hand Blender
Prep: 15 minutes; Cooking: 35 to 40 minutes   Do not freeze   Serves 6 to 8

2 tablespoons vegetable oil

2 medium onions, chopped

1 small to medium red bell pepper, peeled and diced

3$^1/_2$ cups chicken or vegetable broth

2 medium potatoes, about 12 ounces, peeled and diced

$^1/_2$ to $^3/_4$ cup milk

8 ounces coarsely grated cheddar cheese, about 2$^1/_4$ cups

Salt to taste, about $^1/_4$ to $^1/_2$ teaspoon

$^1/_4$ teaspoon freshly ground black pepper

$^1/_8$ to $^1/_4$ teaspoon cayenne, optional

Homemade bacon bits for garnish, optional

1. In a large pot over medium heat, heat the vegetable oil. Add the onions and bell pepper and sauté, stirring occasionally, until the onions are lightly golden, about 10 to 15 minutes.

2. Add the chicken broth and potatoes. Cover and simmer until the potatoes are tender, about 25 to 30 minutes.

3. Puree in batches in a food processor or blender until smooth. Alternatively, if you have a hand blender, leave the soup in the pot and blend.

4. Return the soup to the pot over medium-low heat. Add the milk and cheese and stir until the cheese is melted. Thin with additional milk or broth if it's too thick. Season with salt, pepper, and cayenne. Garnish with bacon bits if you want.

Easy Crab Bisque

There's a famous soup in South Carolina, She-Crab Soup, that uses both the crabmeat and its roe. The roe gives the soup its characteristic pale pink color. Here, a little paprika does the trick.

Although it's been cleaned and picked by packers, you should pick over fresh lump crabmeat to remove any extraneous bits of shell that would otherwise spoil the soup.

Easy Crab Bisque

Easy   Prep: 10 to 15 minutes; Cooking: 30 minutes
Freezes well   Serves 6

3 tablespoons butter or margarine

4 scallions, white part only, chopped

$1/2$ teaspoon paprika

3 tablespoons all-purpose flour

$2^1/3$ cups milk, heated

2 tablespoons dry sherry

$1/2$ teaspoon Worcestershire sauce

12 ounces fresh lump crabmeat, picked over, or two 6-ounce cans, drained

$2/3$ to 1 cup cream or half-and-half

Salt to taste, about $1/2$ teaspoon

$1/8$ teaspoon white pepper

$1/8$ to $1/4$ teaspoon cayenne

1. In a large pot over medium heat, melt the butter. Add the scallions, and sauté, stirring occasionally, until tender, about 5 minutes. Stir in the paprika.

2. Add the flour and cook, stirring constantly, for 2 to 3 minutes.

3. Gradually add the milk, sherry, and Worcestershire sauce, stirring or whisking often until smooth. Simmer, uncovered, for 10 minutes.

4. Add the crabmeat and simmer, uncovered, for 5 minutes.

5. Add the cream and heat for 5 minutes. Do not allow the soup to boil. Season with salt, white pepper, and cayenne.

Souper Bowl Fact

Manufacturers say that **surimi,** a processed form of white fish (generally pollack), is a replacement for crab. It is not suitable for this soup however.

Easy Lobster Bisque

This extravagant soup featuring lobster and cream is decadently rich and absolutely delicious.

Fresh, cooked lobster meat is available in the seafood departments of many supermarkets and fish shops.

Easy Lobster Bisque

Easy   Prep: 10 to 15 minutes; Cooking: 30 minutes
Freezes well   Serves 4 to 6

3 tablespoons butter or margarine

4 scallions, white part only, chopped

$3/4$ teaspoon paprika

3 tablespoons all-purpose flour

$2^1/_3$ cups milk, heated

2 tablespoons dry white vermouth or 1 tablespoon bourbon

$1/2$ teaspoon Worcestershire sauce

12 ounces cooked chopped or shredded lobster meat

$2/3$ to 1 cup cream or half-and-half

Salt to taste, about $1/2$ teaspoon

$1/8$ teaspoon white pepper

1. In a large pot over medium heat, melt the butter. Add the scallions, and sauté, stirring occasionally, until tender, about 5 minutes. Stir in the paprika.

2. Add the flour and cook, stirring constantly, for 2 to 3 minutes.

3. Gradually add the milk, vermouth, and Worcestershire sauce, stirring or whisking often until smooth. Simmer, uncovered, for 10 minutes.

4. Add the lobster and simmer, uncovered, for 5 minutes.

5. Add the cream and heat for 5 minutes. Do not allow the soup to boil. Season with salt and white pepper.

Barbara's Canned Salmon Bisque

Barbara's Canned Salmon Bisque

Food Processor, Blender, or Hand Blender
Prep: 10 minutes; Cooking 40 to 50 minutes   Freezes well   Serves 4 to 6

2 tablespoons butter or margarine	1 bay leaf
3 medium leeks, white part only, sliced	1 teaspoon paprika
1 medium onion, chopped	12 to 14 ounces canned salmon, drained
1 tablespoon tomato paste	
1/2 cup dry white wine or vermouth	Salt to taste, about 1/2 teaspoon
2 1/2 cups homemade fish, vegetable, or chicken broth	1/2 teaspoon freshly ground black pepper
2 cups milk or half-and-half	1 tablespoon chopped fresh parsley, chives, or dill
1 large potato, about 6 to 8 ounces, peeled and diced	

1. In a large pot over medium heat, melt the butter. Add the leeks and onion and sauté until very tender, about 10 minutes.

2. Add the tomato paste and cook, stirring, for 1 minute. Add the wine and cook, stirring for 2 minutes. Add the broth, milk, potato, bay leaf, and paprika. Simmer, partially covered, until the potatoes are tender, about 25 to 30 minutes.

3. Reduce the heat to medium-low. Add the salmon and heat through, about 5 to 7 minutes.

4. Remove the bay leaf. Puree in batches in a blender or food processor until a chunky puree forms. Alternatively, if you have a hand blender, leave the soup in the pot and blend.

5. Return the soup to the pot and reheat over medium heat.

Season with salt and pepper. Serve garnished with parsley, chives or dill.

Souper Bowl Fact

High in protein, salmon is not only a good source of vitamins A and B, but also is rich in omega 3 fatty acids.

The Least You Need to Know

➤ Cream soups should be velvety smooth.

➤ Most cream soups are thickened with a vegetable puree. A modest amount of cream or milk is added for flavor.

➤ Thin cream soups with extra broth, cream, or milk if they're too thick.

➤ Cream soups add extra calcium to your diet.

Chill Out

Who doesn't need to chill out in the summer heat? Fabulous warm weather fare, cold soups are the perfect light meal when the mercury rises. Pair them with bread and salad or use them as a starter followed by a piece of grilled chicken, or fish. The fruit soups can be served either as a light lunch or first course in summer or as a unusual dessert year-round.

Simple and quick to prepare, the only trick is to refrigerate them long enough so they're icy cold. All can be made several hours or up to a day ahead.

Cucumber Soup

This is one of the most refreshing soups for a hot summer day.

To remove the seeds from a cucumber easily, slice the cucumber in half horizontally, then in half lengthwise. Scoop out the seeds with the metal handle of a vegetable peeler, a small melon baller, or a teaspoon.

Cucumber Soup

Easy   Food Processor or Blender
Prep: 15 minutes; Chilling: 1½ to 2 hours   Do not freeze   Serves 6

2 English cucumbers, unpeeled, seeded and coarsely chopped

6 scallions, white part only, thinly sliced

3 cups buttermilk

1 cup plain yogurt

Juice of 1 lemon

1 plump clove garlic, finely minced or pressed

1½ tablespoons fresh dill or mint, minced

Salt to taste, about ½ teaspoon

¼ teaspoon white pepper

1. In a food processor or blender, combine the cucumbers and scallions and puree until smooth.

2. Add the buttermilk, yogurt, lemon juice, garlic, dill, salt, and pepper to the food processor or blender. Pulse until thoroughly mixed.

3. Chill thoroughly. Garnish with extra dill.

Avocado Soup

Versions of this soup can be found from California to the Caribbean, Mexico, and Southern Africa. Make sure you use very ripe avocados in this buttery-textured soup.

Avocado Soup

Easy   Food Processor or Blender
Prep: 15 minutes; Chilling: 1½ to 2 hours   Do not freeze   Serves 6

2 ripe medium avocados, peeled, pit removed

1 tablespoon fresh lemon juice

1 small cucumber, peeled, seeded, and cubed

1 plump clove garlic, finely minced

2 tablespoons minced fresh basil or chives

2¼ cups chicken broth, chilled

⅔ cup plain yogurt or sour cream

Salt to taste, about ½ teaspoon

1. Cube the avocado, put the pulp in a bowl, and toss with the lemon juice.

2. In a food processor, combine the avocado, cucumber, garlic, and basil and puree until smooth.

3. Add the chicken broth and yogurt and pulse until blended.

4. Season with salt. Chill thoroughly.

To prevent avocado flesh from discoloring: immediately after cutting, sprinkle it evenly with a little lemon juice. If the avocado is sliced or cubed, toss gently.

Watercress or Swiss Chard Soup

Watercress has a slightly bitter, peppery bite. Swiss chard is a milder green whose slightly bittersweet taste is reminiscent of spinach and beets. Both work equally well in this recipe.

To store watercress, put the stems in a glass of water, cover with a plastic bag, and refrigerate for up to 3 days. To store Swiss chard, keep in a plastic bag in the refrigerator for up to 3 days. Wash and remove any tough stems before using.

Watercress or Swiss Chard Soup

Easy   Food Processor, Blender, or Hand Blender
Prep: 25 minutes; Chilling: 1¹/₂ to 2 hours   Do not freeze   Serves 4 to 6

2 tablespoons butter, margarine, or vegetable oil

4 medium leeks, white part only, thinly sliced, or 1 small onion, chopped

3 cups chicken or vegetable broth

1 medium potato, peeled and very thinly sliced, about 1¹/₃ cups

¹/₂ bay leaf

1 medium bunch watercress, stems removed, or 3 cups shredded Swiss chard, coarse stems removed

Salt to taste, about ¹/₂ teaspoon

¹/₂ teaspoon black pepper

1¹/₃ cups plain yogurt

1. In a large pot over medium-low heat, melt the butter. Add the leeks and sauté, stirring occasionally, until softened about 5 to 7 minutes.

2. Add the chicken broth, potato, and bay leaf. Increase the heat to medium, cover, and bring the liquid to a boil.

3. Add the watercress or Swiss chard and simmer, covered, until the potato and watercress are tender, about 10 minutes.

4. Cool the soup slightly. Remove the bay leaf. Puree the mixture in batches in a blender or food processor. Alternatively, if you have a hand blender, leave the mixture in the pot and blend.

5. Transfer the puree to a bowl. Taste and season with salt and pepper. Do not add any salt if using Swiss chard. Cool the soup to lukewarm.

6. Stir in the yogurt and chill thoroughly, about 1¹/₂ to 2 hours.

Lemony Minted Green Pea Soup

In the dog days of summer, this marvelous, fresh-tasting soup is superb. In cooler weather, it can be served hot.

Although this soup can be made with a food processor, it is smoother when pureed in a blender or with a hand blender or old-fashioned food mill.

When recipes call for fresh mint, they are referring to spearmint. There are several varieties of mint, such as peppermint and wintergreen, whose flavor is too strong for most savory recipes.

Lemony Minted Green Pea Soup

Easy   Blender or Hand Blender
Prep/Cooking: 25 to 30 minutes; Chilling: 1$^1/_2$ to 2 hours   Freezes well   Serves 6

2 tablespoons butter or margarine

1 medium onion, chopped

1 plump clove garlic, minced

3 cups chicken broth

3$^3/_4$ cups fresh or frozen peas

1 cup fresh mint leaves, minced (about $^1/_4$ cup when minced)

1 teaspoon finely grated lemon zest

1$^1/_4$ cups half-and-half or cream

Salt to taste, about $^1/_2$ teaspoon

$^1/_4$ teaspoon black pepper

Fresh mint sprigs for garnish, optional

1. In a large pot over medium heat, melt the butter. Add the onion and sauté, stirring occasionally, until lightly golden, about 10 to 15 minutes. Add the garlic and cook, stirring occasionally, for 2 minutes.

2. Add the chicken broth and peas and bring the liquid to a boil. Reduce the heat to medium-low and simmer for 5 to 10 minutes until the peas are cooked. Add the mint leaves and cook for 2 minutes.

3. Strain the solids, reserving the broth. In a blender, puree the peas in batches with a small amount of broth until smooth. Alternatively, if you have a hand blender, remove and reserve $^1/_2$ cup of broth and blend the remaining mixture in the pot. Thin with the remaining $^1/_2$ cup of broth if the soup's too thick.

4. In a large bowl combine the peas, lemon zest, and half-and-half. Stir in enough of the reserved broth to make the desired consistency, about 2$^1/_2$ cups. Thin with additional broth if the soup is too thick. Season with salt and pepper.

5. Chill thoroughly, about 2 hours. Garnish with mint leaves.

Vichyssoise

Some restaurants serve this classic soup in a bowl set over a slightly larger bowl of crushed ice. Serve it well chilled, always garnished with chopped chives.

Vichyssoise

Easy   Food Processor, Blender, or Hand Blender
Prep/Cooking: 50 to 60 minutes; Chilling: 2 to 3 hours   Do not freeze   Serves 6

2 tablespoons butter

4 medium leeks, white part only, thinly sliced

1 small onion, thinly sliced

3 cups chicken broth

1^1/$_2$ pounds potatoes, about 3 medium, peeled and thinly sliced

Salt to taste, about ^{1}/$_2$ to ^{3}/$_4$ teaspoon

^{1}/$_8$ teaspoon white pepper

1^1/$_4$ to 1^1/$_2$ cups cream or half-and-half

Chopped chives for garnish

1. In a large pot over medium-low heat, melt the butter. Add the leeks and onion and sauté, stirring occasionally, until lightly golden, about 10 to 15 minutes.

2. Add the broth and potatoes. Increase the heat to medium and bring the liquid to a boil. Simmer, partially covered, until the potatoes are tender, about 25 to 30 minutes.

3. Puree in batches in a food processor or blender until smooth. Alternatively, if you have a hand blender, leave the soup in the pot and blend.

4. Transfer the soup to a large bowl. Add salt to taste and pepper. Thin with the cream and stir to blend.

5. Chill thoroughly, at least 2 hours. Serve garnished with chopped chives.

Souper Bowl Fact

The ultimate potato soup, Vichyssoise (pronounced *vee-shee-swahz*) was the creation of a French chef, Louis Diat, at New York's Ritz-Carlton Hotel in the early 1900s.

Spanish Gazpacho

Gazpacho, the quintessential summer soup from the Andalusia area of Southern Spain, has many versions. This splendid rendition is tangy and slightly chunky.

To cut down on the chilling time, refrigerate the tomato juice and vegetables ahead of time.

Spanish Gazpacho

Easy   Food Processor
Prep: 20 minutes; Chilling: 1¹/₂ to 2 hours   Do not freeze   Serves 6

5 ripe tomatoes, peeled, seeded, and coarsely chopped

1 medium cucumber, peeled, seeded, and coarsely chopped

1 medium green bell pepper, seeded, and coarsely chopped

5 scallions, white and green parts, thinly sliced

1 to 2 jalapeño peppers, seeded and finely minced

2 plump cloves garlic, minced

3 tablespoons minced flat-leaf parsley

1¹/₂ tablespoons minced fresh basil, cilantro, or mint

1¹/₂ cups tomato juice

3 tablespoons red wine vinegar

3 tablespoons extra-virgin olive oil

Salt to taste, about 1 to 1¹/₂ teaspoons

Homemade croutons or croutes for garnish, optional

1. In a large bowl, combine the tomatoes, cucumber, bell pepper, scallions, jalapeño, garlic, parsley, and basil.

2. Put half the vegetable mixture in a food processor and pulse several times until it forms a coarse puree. Set aside.

3. In a large liquid measuring cup, combine the tomato juice, vinegar, olive oil, and salt. Pour into the bowl with the solid vegetables. Return the pureed vegetables to the bowl and stir to mix.

4. Chill thoroughly, about 2 hours. Serve garnished with croutons, if you want, or with croutes on the side.

Carrot Ginger Soup

Chock full of ginger flavor, this zesty soup has been one of my favorites for years. It's terrific cold, but is equally delightful when served piping hot.

For a richer taste, thin this soup with $1/3$ to $1/2$ cup of cream or, to add a more Southeast Asian flair, use unsweetened canned coconut milk. Do not freeze if using coconut milk.

Carrot Ginger Soup

Easy   Food Processor, Blender, or Hand Blender
Prep: 10 to 15 minutes; Cooking: 45 to 50 minutes; Chilling: 2 to 3 hours
Freezes well (but not if you use coconut milk)   Serves 6

2 tablespoons butter or margarine

1 medium onion, chopped

$1^1/_2$ tablespoons minced ginger, about 1- to $1/_2$-inch piece

$1/_4$ teaspoon ground coriander or $1/_8$ teaspoon ground nutmeg

5 cups chicken broth

$1^1/_2$ pounds carrots, peeled and coarsely chopped

Salt to taste, about $1/_2$ teaspoon

Chopped fresh cilantro for garnish

1. In a large pot over medium heat, melt the butter. Add the onion and ginger and sauté, stirring occasionally, until almost tender, about 7 minutes. Add the coriander and cook, stirring occasionally, for 1 minute.

2. Add the chicken broth and carrots. Bring the liquid to a boil. Cover partially and cook until the carrots are tender, about 35 to 40 minutes.

3. Strain, reserving the broth. Puree the vegetables with a small amount of the broth in batches in a food processor or blender until very smooth. Alternatively, if you have a hand blender, leave the soup in the pot and blend.

4. In a large bowl, combine the pureed vegetables with the broth. Season with salt. Chill thoroughly at least 2 hours. Thin, if desired, with additional chilled broth, or with milk or half-and-half. Serve garnished with chopped fresh cilantro.

Cold Sorrel or Spinach Soup

Readily available in spring, sorrel, a leafy green with a somewhat tart and sour taste, is delicious when mellowed in a creamy soup. If it's out of season, substitute spinach and add a tablespoon of fresh lemon juice.

Cold Sorrel or Spinach Soup

Easy   Food Processor, Blender, or Hand Blender
Prep/Cooking: 30 to 35 minutes; Chilling: 2 to 3 hours   Serves 6

2 tablespoons butter

5 scallions, sliced

1 medium potato, peeled and cut in ½-inch chunks

4 cups chicken or vegetable broth

1 pound sorrel, washed and coarsely chopped

¼ teaspoon white pepper

Salt to taste, about ½ teaspoon

1 cup cream, sour cream, or nonfat sour cream

Snipped fresh dill or chopped chives for garnish

1. In a large pot over medium heat, melt the butter. Add the scallions and sauté, stirring occasionally, until tender, about 5 minutes. Add the potatoes and cook, stirring occasionally, for 5 minutes.

2. Add the broth and sorrel. Bring to a boil and cook until the potatoes and sorrel are tender, about 15 to 20 minutes.

3. Puree in batches in a blender or food processor until smooth. Alternatively, if you have a hand blender, leave the soup in the pot and blend.

4. Transfer to a bowl and add the pepper and salt. Chill thoroughly, at least 2 hours.

5. Before serving, stir in the cream or sour cream and garnish with fresh dill.

Souper Bowl Fact

Leafy greens, such as sorrel, Swiss chard, and spinach, are an excellent source of Vitamins A and C, and are rich in iron.

Very Berry Fruit Gazpacho

A combination of berries creates this delectable, fragrantly spiced fruit soup. A cooling and refreshing soup indeed!

Wrap the whole spices in cheesecloth to form a bouquet garni that can be removed easily from the soup before pureeing.

Usually more tart than overly sweet, fruit soups are typical of Scandinavian fare. Recipes were brought by immigrants to the United States. Although they are most often served cold, they can also be served hot.

Very Berry Fruit Gazpacho

Easy to Intermediate   Food Processor, Blender, or Hand Blender
Prep/Cooking: 20 to 25 minutes; Chilling: 2 to 3 hours
Freezes well without diced fruit   Serves 4 to 6

4 to 5 cups mixed unsweetened frozen or fresh berries, such as blueberries, blackberries, sliced strawberries, raspberries, or pitted cherries

2 cups water

$1/2$ cup ruby port or red wine, optional

$2/3$ to 1 cup sugar, or to taste

2 allspice berries or whole cloves

1 cinnamon stick

1 small, quarter-sized slice of fresh ginger

$1^1/_2$ cups diced fruit such as kiwi, pineapple, mango, papaya, or strawberries, optional

Mint leaves for garnish

Whipped cream or yogurt, for garnish, optional

1. In a large pot over medium heat, combine the berries, water, port, sugar, allspice, cinnamon, and ginger. Cover and bring the liquid to a boil. Reduce the heat to medium-low and simmer, uncovered, until the berries are very soft, about 10 to 15 minutes. Taste for sugar, adding more if you want.

2. With a slotted spoon, remove the whole spices and ginger. Puree the mixture in batches in a food processor or blender until smooth. Alternatively, if you have a hand blender, leave the soup in the pot and blend.

3. Strain through a fine-mesh sieve into a clean bowl to remove seeds, pressing lightly on the sieve with the back of a spoon.

4. Chill thoroughly, at least 2 hours.

5. To serve, divide the diced fruit among bowls and ladle the soup on top. Garnish with mint leaves and a dollop of whipped cream or yogurt.

Cantaloupe Orange Soup

Good for brunch, lunch, dinner, or dessert, this light soup can be made in a flash.

If you're planning to make this soup, refrigerate the melon overnight. Chilling time will be cut in half, but it will still be long enough to allow the flavors to blend fully.

Cantaloupe Orange Soup

Easy   Food Processor or Blender
Prep: 10 minutes; Chilling: 1¹/₂ to 2 hours   Do not freeze   Serves 6 to 8

3 medium or 2 large very ripe cantaloupes, peeled, seeded, and cut into chunks

1¹/₄ cups chilled fresh orange juice

Juice of 1 medium lemon or lime

¹/₄ to ¹/₃ cup sherry or additional orange juice

Finely grated zest of one small orange

2 to 3 tablespoons sugar, optional

¹/₂ teaspoon ground coriander, optional

Pinch of salt

3 tablespoons chopped fresh mint, optional

1. In a food processor or blender, puree the cantaloupe. Add the orange juice, lemon juice, and sherry. Pulse until smooth.

2. Transfer the soup to a bowl. Stir in the orange zest, sugar, coriander, and salt. Thin with additional orange juice, if necessary. Chill thoroughly, about 1¹/₂ hours. Stir in the mint right before serving.

The Least You Need to Know

➤ Make the soup ahead of time so you have enough time to chill it adequately.

➤ Chill the soup bowls for an especially nice presentation.

➤ Thin chilled soup with cold broth, milk, or juice.

Chapter 21

Fast Finishes

In This Chapter

➤ Bacon Bits

➤ Pesto

➤ Croutes and Croutons

➤ Oven-Toasted Bread

Garnishes are your closing statement—the finale of the dish. Although much of the time you'll use chopped fresh herbs or nothing at all, in this chapter you'll find easy recipes to make your presentation a bit more appetizing.

Bacon Bits

Freshly cooked bacon bits are a wonderful addition to many soups.

Make the bacon bits a day or two ahead of time and store them in an airtight container in the refrigerator. Bring them to room temperature before using.

Bacon Bits

Easy   10 to 15 minutes   Do not freeze

6 slices of bacon, preferably thick-cut,
or 6 slices slab bacon, rind removed

1. Cut the bacon slices crosswise into thin strips, about $1/4$- to $1/2$-inch thick.

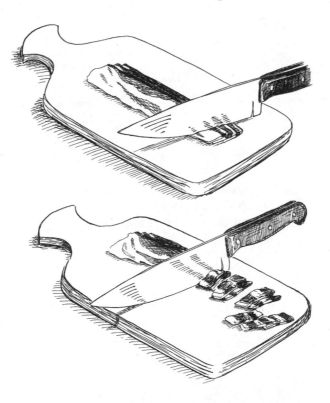

2. Cook in a medium skillet over medium-low heat, stirring occasionally, until the bacon bits begin to brown on all sides. With a slotted spoon, transfer the bacon to a paper towel-lined plate and blot off the excess fat.

Pesto

Pesto isn't just for pasta. It is also a lovely complement to many tomato-based and vegetable soups.

Put extra pesto in an airtight plastic container and cover the top of the pesto with a thin layer of olive oil. Store in the refrigerator for 2 to 4 weeks or freeze for up to 3 months. Allow the pesto to come to room temperature before using it in any recipe. You can use leftover pesto on pasta or as a garnish for sliced mozzarella and tomato salad, or on roasted bell pepper salad.

Try making pesto with other herbs, such as flat-leaf Italian parsley or cilantro. If using parsley, add the finely grated zest of $1/2$ medium lemon. Use this pesto in place of basil pesto. If using cilantro, omit the Parmesan and use $1/3$ cup walnuts and $1/3$ to $1/2$ cup olive oil. Add 1 to 2 seeded and minced jalapeño or serrano chilies and use for Mexican, Latin American, or even Southeast Asian dishes.

Pesto

Easy   Food Processor or Blender
10 to 15 minutes   Freezes well

2 cups fresh basil leaves
$1/4$ cup pine nuts or chopped walnuts
2 to 3 cloves garlic, peeled
$1/3$ cup freshly grated Parmesan cheese

$1/8$ teaspoon freshly ground black pepper
$1/2$ cup extra-virgin olive oil

1. In a food processor or blender combine the basil, pine nuts, and garlic. Pulse until the ingredients form a paste. Add the Parmesan cheese and pepper and pulse until blended.
2. While the machine is running, pour the olive oil through the feeding tube. If you're using a blender, remove the plastic handle from the top of the blender, replace the top on the machine and pour the olive oil through the hole. If the pesto is a bit too thick, gradually add a bit more olive oil.

Baked Croutes or Croutons

Croutes and croutons are traditionally used in many soups, hors d'oeuvres, and salads.

To make croutes or croutons oil free: Preheat oven to 200°F. Put the croutes or croutons on a baking sheet and bake, turning once, until dried out.

Baked Croutes or Croutons

Easy   15 minutes   Do not freeze

For Croutes: Use French or Italian bread or sourdough bread. In a pinch, you can use any tightly grained white bread.

Preheat oven to 375°F. Cut the bread into slices about $1/2$- to $3/4$-inch thick.

Brush the bread slices lightly with olive oil and arrange in a single layer on a baking sheet.

Bake, turning once, until lightly golden and crisp, about 8 to 12 minutes.

For Croutons: Use French, sourdough, Italian, or simple white or whole wheat loaf bread.

Preheat oven to 375°F. Cut bread into cubes.

Put a small amount of olive oil in a bowl. Toss the bread in the olive oil.

Arrange in a single layer on a baking sheet and bake, turning once, until lightly golden and crisp, about 8 to 12 minutes.

For Herbed Croutes or Croutons: Add a small amount of dried herbs, such as basil, thyme, or crushed rosemary, to the olive oil you will use to brush onto the croutes or toss the croutons in.

Oven-Toasted Bread

This is an easy way to toast bread that is too thick or the wrong shape for your toaster. You can also make more than 2 or 4 slices at a time.

Crush extra toast into bread crumbs and store in an airtight container in the refrigerator for up to 2 weeks.

Oven-Toasted Bread

Easy   5 to 10 minutes   Do not freeze

1. Preheat oven to 375° to 400°F. Place bread slices on a baking sheet and bake until lightly toasted, turning once.

The Least You Need to Know

➤ Garnishes add a final sparkle to any dish.

➤ Keep garnishes simple.

➤ Prepare garnishes ahead and set them aside.

➤ Add garnishes right before serving.

The Complete Idiot's Soup Reference Guide

Souper Cooking Lingo

Chop   To cut into irregularly shaped pieces of uniform size. Chopped ingredients are $1/4$ to $1/2$ inch.

Cube   To cut into pieces of uniform shape and size. Cubes sizes are indicated and can range from $1/2$ inch up to 2 inches.

Dice   To cut into small pieces of uniform size and shape. Diced ingredients are $1/4$ inch up to $1/2$ inch.

Mince   To cut into irregularly shaped pieces less than $1/8$ inch in size.

Puree   To blend food until smooth or slightly chunky, according to the recipe.

Sauté   To cook over medium to medium-high heat in a small amount of fat. Don't crowd the pan.

Simmer   To cook over medium-low to low heat so the liquid gently bubbles.

Soup-Making Hints

➤ First comes your *mise en place*. It's easy: assemble all your equipment and prep all the ingredients before you start to cook.

➤ Cut like ingredients in similar size pieces for even cooking.

➤ Before you begin to cook, read the recipe again thoroughly to familiarize yourself with the process.

➤ Sometimes you'll sauté first, sometimes you won't.

➤ Simmer soup, don't boil it.

➤ Add additional liquid if too much evaporates and the soup is too thick.

➤ Puree food in batches in a food processor or blender, or use a hand blender right in the soup pot.

Soup Safety Tips

➤ When storing leftover soup and broth, cool quickly by stirring or putting in sink partially filled with iced water.

➤ To freeze soup, first cool it, then freeze in a freezer-proof container.

➤ Fill storage containers completely but leave $1/2$-inch breathing or expansion room.

Basic Measurement Guide

1 tablespoon = 3 teaspoons

$1/2$ tablespoon = $1^1/2$ teaspoons

$1/4$ cup = 4 tablespoons

$1/3$ cup = $5^1/2$ tablespoons

$1/2$ cup = 8 tablespoons

8 ounces liquid = 1 cup

16 ounces liquid = 1 pint = 2 cups

32 ounces liquid = 1 quart = 4 cups or 2 pints

4 ounces = $1/4$ pound

8 ounces = $1/2$ pound

16 ounces = 1 pound

Measurement Abbreviations

Tablespoon = TBS, Tbs., Tbl., T

Teaspoon = tsp., t.

Cup = c.

Pint = pt.

Quart = qt.

Ounce = oz.

Pound = lb.

Measuring Common Ingredients

1 plump clove garlic = $1/2$ teaspoon, minced

1-inch finger ginger = 1 tablespoon, minced

1 teaspoon fresh herbs, minced = $1/2$ teaspoon dried

1 medium tomato, peeled, seeded, and chopped = $1/2$ cup

1 plum tomato, peeled, seeded, and chopped = $1/4$ to $1/3$ cup

1 cup dry beans or lentils = approximately $3^1/4$ to $3^1/2$ cups cooked or canned, drained

One 15- to 16-ounce can of beans, drained = $1^1/2$ to $1^3/4$ cups

Index